IMAGES
of America

Hawai'i Volcanoes National Park

On the Cover: An explosion at Halemaumau Crater creates a rising fume cloud—seen from Volcano House—at 8:30 a.m., on May 22, 1924. The cloud was an estimated two-and-one-third miles in height. The eruption, which began on May 18, 1924, was highly explosive. Huge boulders, weighing several tons, were thrown from the crater and crashed to the floor as ash and pumice filled the air. This eruption of the usually mild Kilauea Volcano reminded everyone that it is, in fact, an explosive volcano and potentially lethal. (Courtesy of Hawai'i Volcanoes National Park.)

IMAGES
of America

Hawai'i Volcanoes National Park

Jeanette Foster

ARCADIA
PUBLISHING

ISBN 978-1-4671-3294-7

Published by Arcadia Publishing
Charleston, South Carolina

Printed in the United States of America

Library of Congress Control Number: 2014947372

For all general information, please contact Arcadia Publishing:
Telephone 843-853-2070
Fax 843-853-0044
E-mail sales@arcadiapublishing.com
For customer service and orders:
Toll-Free 1-888-313-2665

Visit us on the Internet at www.arcadiapublishing.com

This book is dedicated to the continued inspiration from the Hawaii volcano goddess, Pele, and her grandmother, Kamehae.

Contents

ACKNOWLEDGMENTS

The Hawai'i Volcanoes National Park's (HVNP) archives of historic photographs are an incredible resource of images that trace the history of the park through luau celebrations, pageants to Pele, and volcanic eruptions. All of the images used in this book came from their archives.

I am grateful for the aloha and help that I received from Tracy A. Laqua, museum curator for the Hawai'i Volcanoes National Park, and for her volunteers, who scanned selected images. I could not have finished this book without the helping hand of Jessica Ferracane, the public affairs specialist for the park. Finally, I am very appreciative of the support of park superintendent Cindy Orlando in the creation of the book.

I would like to give a big *mahalo* (thank you) to the hardworking scientists and staff at the Hawaiian Volcano Observatory for their dedicated study of the volcanoes, their incredible collection of data, and their remarkable innovations that have made life in Hawaii much safer.

I also want to thank my editor at Arcadia Publishing, Ginny Rasmussen, for her expert guidance.

INTRODUCTION

It was the fire in the sky that drew them.

The legends spoke of islands far, far away, that lit up the dark night skies. Brave open-ocean voyagers left their Polynesian homes and ventured into unknown waters, looking for a mythical land that was lit by fire.

The islands were the most isolated on earth—located more than 2,000 miles from the nearest continent. Today, it is still unknown when the first Polynesian voyagers set foot on Hawaii. Some claim that it was 700 years ago, others say 1,000 years or even longer. Regardless, legends state that the Polynesians were guided by the light—the fire—of the erupting volcanoes.

Legends also tell the story of Pele, the goddess of the volcano, who ventured to Hawaii looking for a home after the land was formed. She settled in the Kilauea Crater, on the island of Hawaii, where she remains today. Even today, Hawaiians point to photographs of lava eruptions that form the faint outline of a woman's face and tell stories of an old (or young) woman walking alone in the dark.

For generations, people have been drawn to these erupting volcanoes. The first written description of the Kilauea eruption comes from a 1794 journal of Archibald Menzies, the naturalist aboard Capt. George Vancouver's ship, *Discovery*.

It was William Ellis, however—a missionary with the London Mission Society—who described his astonishment over the 1823 eruption of Kilauea as he stood "with wonder on the edge of its ancient craters, walked tremblingly along the brink of its smoking chasms, gazed with admiration on its raging fires, and witnessed, with no ordinary feelings of awe, the varied and sublime phenomena of volcanic action, in all its imposing magnificence and terrific grandeur."

Upon seeing Kilauea in 1866, experienced world traveler Mark Twain wrote, "Here was room for the imagination to work!"

Word of this "sublime phenomena" soon got out, but reaching the volcano was difficult. Kilauea was far from the island's population centers—about 30 miles from the port of Hilo, on the eastern coast, and 90 miles from the village of Kona, on the western coast. The area could be reached on horseback via non-maintained, hard-to-follow trails. In 1844, a local resident erected a grass hut on the edge of the crater and began providing food to travelers. In 1846, Benjamin Pitman built the area's first formal accommodations when he constructed Volcano House, which featured single rooms with mats on a dirt floor, on the side of Kilauea Crater.

In 1906, Lorrin A. Thurston, publisher of the *Pacific Commercial Advertiser*, started a campaign to make this amazing resource a public park. Six years later, Dr. Thomas A. Jaggar, a scientist who came to Hawaii to establish and serve as director of the Hawaiian Volcano Observatory, joined efforts with Thurston to convince the public, politicians, and anyone who would listen to protect the volcanoes by making the area a national park.

On August 1, 1916, Pres. Woodrow Wilson signed the country's 13th national park into existence. At the time, the park—which was called Hawaii National Park—consisted of some 35,865 acres around Kilauea, 17,920 acres around the nearby Mauna Loa volcano, and a small strip of land connecting the two volcanoes. The park also included the volcano of Haleakala (which became a national park on August 21, 1961) on the island of Maui. Today, the Hawai'i Volcanoes National Park consists of 333,086 acres located in the southeastern region of the island of Hawaii. The park ranges from the top of Mauna Loa, at 13,677 feet, down to sea level and includes a diverse range of ecosystems, including seacoast, rainforests, woodlands, and alpine reaches. It also includes—as it always has—two of the world's most active volcanoes: Kilauea (which has been erupting nearly continuously since 1983) and Mauna Loa (which last erupted in 1984). Additionally, UNESCO declared the Hawaiian Islands as a Biosphere Reserve in 1980 and designated the park as a World Heritage Site in 1987.

Over the last century, the park has contributed to the science of volcanology by offering scientists a front-row seat to watch erupting volcanoes. The park played a role in the development of a scientific theory regarding volcanoes and tectonic plates in the late 1960s. Some places on the planet contain hot spots—areas where the temperature of molten lava reaches some 7,000 degrees Fahrenheit. The earth consists of constantly shifting tectonic plates. As these tectonic plates passed over the hot spots, volcanoes were formed. In terms of the Hawaiian island chain, the older islands begin at the northwest end of the chain and get younger as one moves south and east toward the island of Hawaii, the youngest and largest, which is estimated to be only one million years old.

Hawai'i Volcanoes National Park also serves ecological and cultural purposes. Ecologically, it is a refuge for endangered species like the *honu 'ea* (hawksbill turtle), *nene* (Hawaiian goose), *'ua'u* (Hawaiian petrel), *'io* (Hawaiian hawk), and *ope'ape'a* (Hawaiian hoary bat). Culturally, the park protects and perpetuates the culture of indigenous Hawaiians.

Every year, 1.5 million visitors make the journey up to the park entrance located 4,000 feet above sea level. There, they can traverse 66 miles of paved roads and 155 miles of marked trails as they experience, "with no ordinary feelings of awe," the miracle of creation as molten lava erupts from within the earth and pours down the side of the mountain.

So it is the fire that continues to draw people. Silhouetted against the fire of the eruption, visitors to the park stand on the edge of the earth—just as the native Hawaiians probably did thousands of years before—drawn there to witness the mountain's dual act of creation and destruction.

Watching the lava at night is perhaps the greatest show on earth; its ruby rivers snake down the volcanic slope, running just below the surface, and then emerge from their subterranean tunnels only to gush into the Pacific Ocean. As the molten rock—still several thousand degrees Fahrenheit—strikes the placid ocean, the air explodes with a symphony of loud pops, guttural hissing, and vociferous crackling. The lava continues to burn in the 77-degree ocean water until the vast Pacific finally douses it, transforming the flow into what will, someday, be a sandy beach.

It is a sight to be remembered.

One

Hawaiian Myths

Hawaiian culture is rich with images and descriptions handed down through the generations via oral histories and legends. Some stories are set to music and dance and have been chanted for centuries. One of the most revered chants is the "Kumulipo," the chant of creation, which speaks about heat forming the earth, corals appearing, and stones breeding more stones.

Many of these stories and chants surround the volcano goddess, Pele. In ancient Hawaii, the gods controlled various aspects of life ranging from the weather to agriculture to fishing. One legend speaks of Pele, along with her sister Hi'iaka, arriving in the Hawaiian islands aboard a canoe sailed by her brother Kamohoalii.

Pele began searching for a home in the Hawaiian Islands by digging for heat and lava. She started at the northern end of the chain on Niihau and tried one island after another but could not find the type of home that she wanted.

Even today, Hawaiians will point to pits, caves, and volcanic cones and say that they are evidence of Pele's search for a home.

When Pele reached the Big Island, some legends say that she met another volcano god, Aila'au, Eater of the Forest. Aila'au lived at Kilauea—in the curtain of fire made from lava fountains—and when he saw Pele coming to the island, Aila'au instantly recognized the new goddess's vastly superior power. Wisely, Aila'au disappeared from the island, leaving behind the heat and lava Pele that was looking for. Stories say that this is where Pele remains, even today.

Pele has a reputation for being a temperamental goddess who expresses her displeasure by sending fiery lava flows to destroy whatever angers her. To please their goddess, Pele's followers frequently brought her offerings—a tradition that still survives among the Hawaiian people.

Before the missionaries brought Christianity to the islands, they contained many worshipers of Pele. In 1824, however, the high chiefess, Kapiolani, converted to Christianity and nearly dealt a fatal blow to the worshippers of the volcano goddess. She confronted Pele at the edge of the Kilauea crater by reading from the Bible, eating Pele's beloved ohelo berries without making an offering of them to the goddess, and throwing stones into the erupting crater. Kapiolani waited for a sign from the goddess—a punishment for her blatant disrespect—but received only silence. Kapiolani remained unpunished, and as a result, she declared Pele defeated.

Ancient Hawaiians did not have a written language, but they did leave several thousand carvings in rocks. Scientists still argue over the meaning of these symbols known as petroglyphs or *ki'i pohaku*. Some suppose that they document important events, like victory in battle or the birth of a person of high rank. Others say they represent detailed histories. Hawai'i Volcanoes National Park visitors can take a short, self-guided hike of one of Hawaii's largest petroglyph fields, the Pu'u Loa Petroglyphs, at the ocean end of Chain of Craters Road.

Followers of Pele believe that she still exists today, pointing to photographs that appear to show the faint outline of a woman, such as the image at right. They also believe that Pele can take human form and walk the earth. One legend tells of Pele approaching two girls cooking breadfruit. Pele, disguised as an old woman, approached the girls and asked for food. One girl was generous and gave Pele a bowlful, but the other girl refused. Pele warned the generous girl that the lava flow was coming, and she was able to leave the area safely. Pele told the second girl nothing, and the girl's family home was destroyed by lava.

A myth about Pele states that she will become very angry if anyone takes anything from the Hawai'i Volcanoes National Park, and that she will put a curse of bad luck on that person for stealing from her. It has been suggested that a park ranger made up this myth to prevent visitors from taking rocks from the park—already an illegal act. Others say this myth was created by a bus driver who was tired of visitors collecting rocks and other debris and carrying them onto his bus. Although a search of Hawaiian myths does not unearth stories about this curse, park officials regularly receive boxes of rocks accompanied by notes claiming that the note-writers have had nothing but bad luck since they took the rocks. Park rangers even have an area where they respectfully return these rocks to the park.

Just like the ancient Hawaiians, visitors to Hawaii are awestruck by the work of Pele when volcanoes are erupting. More than 1.5 million visitors visit Hawai'i Volcanoes National Park every year. The number of visitors to the park is steadily increasing every year. According to a report commissioned by the National Park Service, 1,583,209 people visited the park in 2013—a 6.7 percent increase over 2012. Additionally, those visitors spent more than $124 million in the area—a 10.2 percent increase over 2012.

The report also notes that similar gains have been recorded in each of the past five years. Several factors contributing to the increases were noted by park superintendent Cindy Orlando, who said, "the ease of viewing the summit eruption from Kilauea, the many free cultural and scientific programs, the reopening of Volcano House, and the diverse ecosystem of native plants and animals that park stewards have worked hard to protect for nearly 100 years are part of what attracts people."

This aerial view of the Halemaumau Crater shows the beginning of the 1952 eruption on June 27. A fissure opened across the crater floor, and for the next few hours, a continuous line of lava fountains—some half a mile long—spurted from it. Most of the fountains were 50 to 130 feet high, but at the southwest edge, one fountain rose to more than 800 feet. Fluid lava, pouring out at a rate of 2 million cubic yards per hour, quickly covered the entire crater floor, and, by 4:00 the next morning, the pool of liquid lava was 50 feet deep.

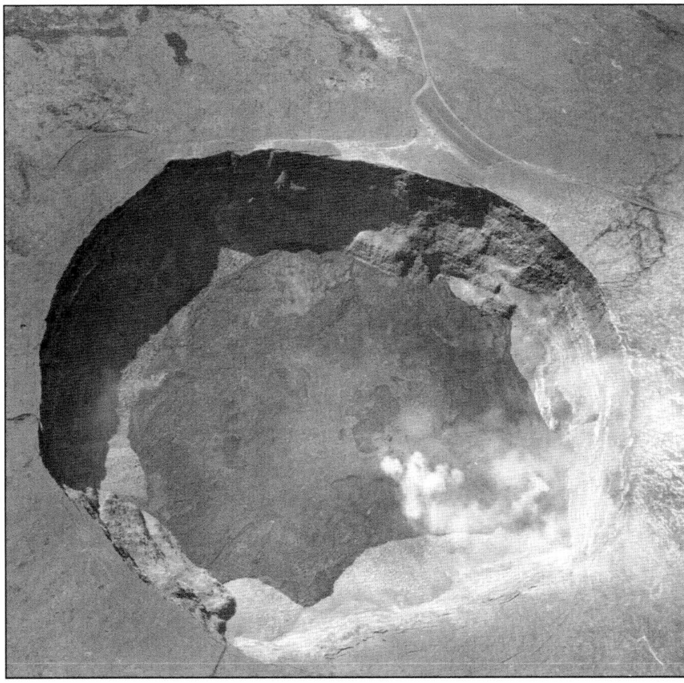

Activity waxed and waned during the 1952 eruption, but it generally decreased until early November. At the southwestern edge of the crater, one spectacular fountain continued for about a week. At certain times, it reached a height of 600 feet; at other times, it died out completely and was replaced by a sinkhole—an effect caused by the liquid lava draining back into the conduit beneath.

This nighttime photograph shows the spectacular fountains of lava that the 1952 eruption was known for. The fountains regularly reached 100 feet in height, with some shooting up to 400 feet. These fountains brought the amount of lava in the lake to about 4 million cubic yards in just the first 30 minutes of the eruption.

Some Hawaiians believe that volcanoes are living things, and some scientists agree that they sometimes act that way. Volcanoes are not static; they are constantly changing and even, as pictured, collapsing. A collapse can be caused by rocks within the vent, lava within the vent continuously circulating a gas-rich "foam" that rises and falls depending on changes in the subsurface magma pressure, or a number of other factors. When a collapse occurs, visitors can see the rising plumes of smoke, hear the thundering landslides, and—occasionally—feel the earth shake.

The volcano goddess, Pele, always seems ready to produce a show for visitors to Hawai'i Volcanoes National Park. Legends of this goddess often center on her passion, her volatility, and her jealousy. One story tells of one of Pele's lovers, Kamapuaa, a demigod who was a pig but hid the bristles that grew down his back by wearing a cape. This pig god could also appear as a plant or as various types of fish. He and Pele had a tumultuous relationship—Pele covered the land with barren lava, and Kamapuaa brought torrents of rain to extinguish her fires before he called the wild boars to dig up the land to soften it so that seeds could grow.

This photograph of Halemaumau shows the crater degassing—the process by which magma loses its volatile substances to the atmosphere. Some of the largest amounts of volcanic degassing occur at lava lakes. Ancient Hawaiians believed that their volcano goddess was angry when they saw this phenomenon.

This photograph shows two men inspecting the steaming crater at Uwekahuna Bluff, which means "weeping of the *kahuna*" or "weeping of the priests." This was the place where Hawaiian priests kept a constant vigil and chanted to appease Pele. It is also the highest point on the caldera wall and overlooks the northern section of the Kilauea caldera. Because of the excellent location, this is where Dr. Thomas Jaggar chose to place the Hawaiian Volcano Observatory and where the National Park Service built the Jaggar Museum.

Hawaiians believed that Pele could be seen rising with the steam at the Kilauea crater. The old Hawaiian religions were abolished around 1820, when missionaries brought Christianity to the island, but worship of Pele is still practiced today—even among some non-Hawaiians. When the Greek-born "Uncle" George Lycurgus ran the Volcano House hotel, he was very vocal about praying for Pele to erupt so that more visitors would flock to Hawai'i Volcanoes National Park and stay at his hotel. Park officials were not thrilled with Lycurgus's practice of tossing gin bottles into the crater and saying that they were offerings to Pele.

The glow from inside the Kilauea crater makes it is easy to understand how Hawaiians believed that Pele lived in the volcano. The ancient Hawaiians developed a highly stratified society on their isolated islands that used a *kapu* (taboo) system to maintain law and order. Under the kapu system, the sovereign *alii* (chiefs) imposed religious and practical beliefs over the entire population. The alii ruled the land, while the *kahuna* (priests) directed religious life, and the *maka'ainana* (commoners) farmed, fished, built structures and fishponds, and paid taxes. The *kaua*, who were considered slaves or outcasts, were the lowest class in this society. Throughout their island villages, Native Hawaiians collected shellfish, seaweed, and salt; raised pigs, dogs, and chickens; and harvested sweet potatoes and taro. The people worshipped the *akua* (gods) and the *aumakua* (guardian spirits), and they passed their cultural traditions to future generations through *oli* (chant), *mele* (song), and *hula* (dance).

Above, steam rises from the Halemaumau Crater after a heavy rainfall. Hawai'i Volcanoes National Park is home to more than just myths and legends—it also features numerous archeological sites (such as the one shown below) and historic districts. These sites pay tribute to the unique Hawaiian culture that developed before Western contact and include petroglyphs, historic trails, fossilized footprints, shelter caves, scattered remains of *heiau* (temple) ruins, house platforms, and the stone walls of canoe sheds, pens, and corrals. Many of these sites are listed in the National Register of Historic Places, as they offer evidence of the thriving *ohana* (family) communities that developed on this lava-touched landscape. The trail system, which includes trails like the Puna-Ka'u Coastal Trail and the Keauhou Trail, connected families living and fishing along the coast with farmers who lived and worked further inland. Native Hawaiians originally used trails to bring offerings to Pele, and visitors can still use portions of these trails to hike to the summit of Mauna Loa.

In 1922, members of the community, including influential community leaders in Honolulu, organized a nonprofit called Hui O Pele Hawaii ("Group for Pele Hawaii") to raise money for services and facilities in the park. Occasionally, the group also acted as an ad hoc adviser to the park superintendent on cultural issues. In 1928, the chairman of Hui O Pele, L.W. De Vis-Norton, wrote a letter to the new park superintendent, Thomas J. Allen Jr., on the practice of hitting golf balls from the rim into the crater, which was popular with visitors, stating: "Most of the Hawaiians have a sincere reverence for Halemaumau. To them, the place is sacred—and they regard the stunt of plugging golf balls into Pele's abode as much as you would view a game of craps played on the grave of the Unknown Soldier at Arlington." A glimpse at the spectacular June 27, 1952, eruption pictured below helps demonstrate why the Hawaiians held Pele in such high esteem.

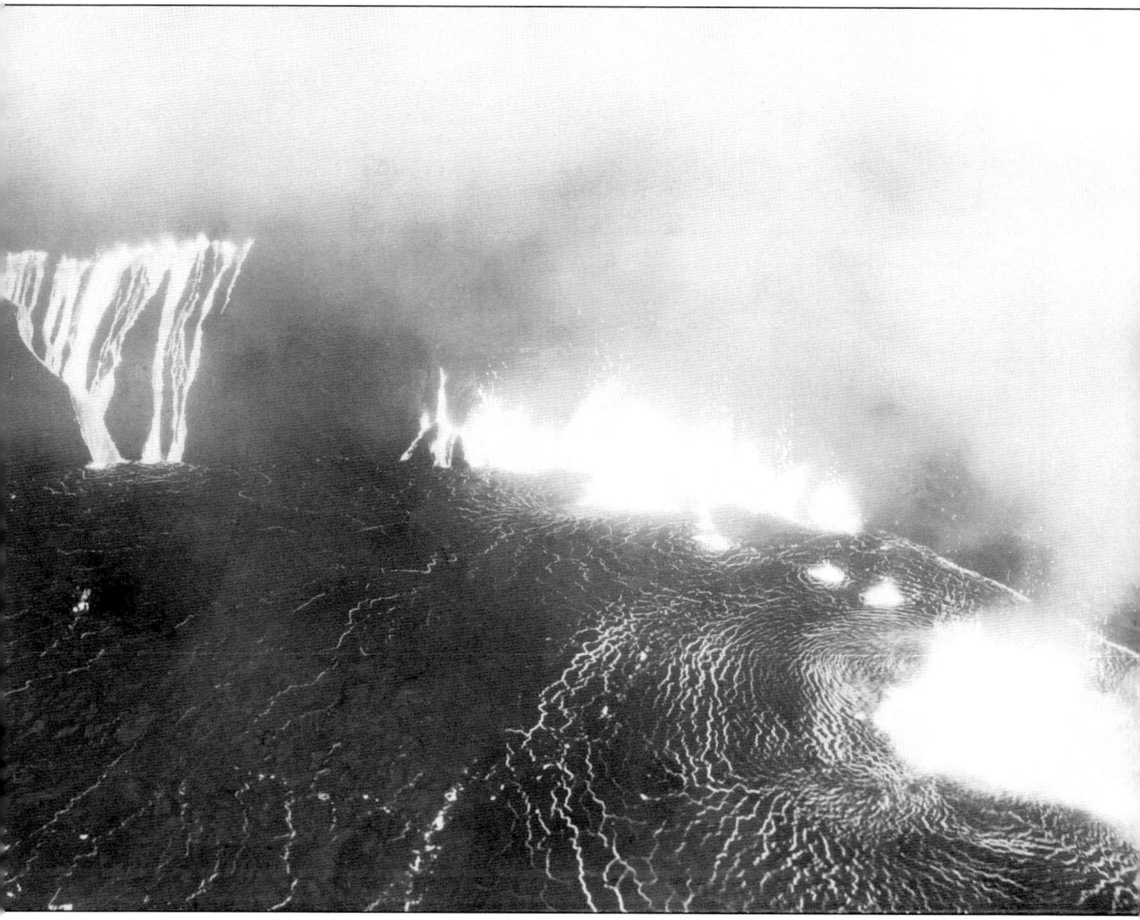

Pele remained quiet from December 1931 until September 1934. Then, at 2:44 a.m. on October 8, 1934, she erupted from the floor of Halemaumau. There had been some indication that the volcano was waking up as rockslides struck the Halemaumau Crater, and on the afternoon of September 5, the Hawaiian Volcano Observatory made note of the southwest tilt of Kilauea's summit. The observatory's seismic instruments recorded spasms of volcanic tremors about an hour before the eruption began. Lava fountains initially erupted at three places within Halemaumau Crater, and a cascade of lava surged from a 900-foot horizontal crack located halfway up the west wall of Halemaumau. Thirty jets of lava shot up from the northwest crater floor, sending fragments of pumice several hundred feet above the crater rim. Lava flows spread across the floor of Halemaumau and coalesced into a glowing lake that quickly submerged the third—and most northern—line of fountains. Within hours, the entire crater floor was covered in lava that was 60 feet deep.

At the time, the 1967–1968 eruption of Kilauea became the longest eruption after lasting for 251 days. The current eruption, which began in January 1983, surpassed that record decades ago.

Two

The Making of a National Park

The ancient Hawaiians understood what an incredible resource the volcanoes were. The area was remote, however, so few Westerners had the opportunity to experience the magnificence of the area.

In 1823, a missionary named William Ellis observed the erupting volcano, and word of this natural phenomenon soon began to spread. Mark Twain visited the territory that would eventually become Hawaii, vividly describing his experience at the 1866 eruption of Kilauea in his 1872 book *Roughing It*.

Unfortunately, it could be difficult to get to the site of the eruption, which was miles from any city, in the mid-19th century. The long, uphill journey—which was made on horseback—followed a course of rough, barely-visible trails. Once a visitor got to the volcano, they generally had to remain overnight. Even then, there were no accommodations available until 1844, when a local set up a grass hut on the edge of the crater. A couple of years later, Benjamin Pitman constructed the first Volcano House, which featured single rooms, mats, and dirt floors.

For 10 years, Lorrin A. Thurston, publisher of the *Pacific Commercial Advertiser*, and Dr. Thomas A. Jaggar, director of the Hawaiian Volcano Observatory, lobbied to get the area preserved as a national park. On August 1, 1916, Pres. Woodrow Wilson signed the country's 13th national park into existence. Hawaii National Park encompassed the summits of Kilauea and Mauna Loa, on the island of Hawaii, as well as the summit of Haleakala, on the island of Maui. In 1961, Haleakala became a separate national park, and the land on the island of Hawaii became Hawai'i Volcanoes National Park.

After a decade of lobbying from Lorrin A. Thurston, publisher of the *Pacific Commercial Advertiser*, and Dr. Thomas A. Jaggar, director of the Hawaiian Volcano Observatory, Pres. Woodrow Wilson finally dedicated the area around the volcanoes as Hawaii National Park on August 1, 1916. This first park included the volcanoes on the island of Hawaii as well as the volcano Haleakala on Maui. In 1961, each island got its own national park—Haleakala National Park on Maui and Hawai'i Volcanoes National Park on Hawaii. In 1980, the United Nations Educational, Scientific, and Cultural Organization (UNESCO) named the Hawaiian Islands a Biosphere Reserve due to the area's incredible cultural and scientific resources. In 1987, the organization recognized the importance of the park by naming it as a World Heritage Site for its natural, historical, and cultural value to all people of the planet.

Once the area surrounding the Kilauea and Mauna Loa volcanoes became a national park, staff members faced the challenge of building and maintaining park structures and roads. Due to its remote location, high-altitude mountains, rugged terrain, and erupting volcanoes, creating this infrastructure was a slow, arduous procedure. Some of these difficulties persist today, as the slopes of the 13,677-foot Mauna Loa are covered with snow during the winter months, and pack horses are still used to deliver construction material to hard-to-reach locations. These issues are compounded by volcanic eruptions, which send out lava flows that cut off access to roads, destroy structures, and makes accessibility difficult at best.

Lorrin A. Thurston, publisher of the *Pacific Commercial Advertiser*, loved the area around Kilauea Crater and was an ardent hiker and intrepid explorer of the area. Among his various discoveries was a giant lava tube that formed when a river of molten lava cooled down and crusted over while the still-hot liquid interior continued to flow down the side of the mountain. Eventually, the liquid lava drained out of the tube, leaving a cave-like shell. Now known as the Thurston Lava Tube (left), it remains a popular attraction in the park. The trail from the parking area to the tube, called the Thurston Lava Tube Trail (below), is surrounded by lush ferns.

Three

Volcanology and Its Role in the Park

In 1912, Dr. Thomas A. Jaggar—who had three degrees from Harvard and was the head of the Massachusetts Institute of Technology's geology department—was frustrated. He felt his field of volcanology was being stifled because no academic center in the United States had an on-site volcano observatory.

Jaggar bemoaned the fact that there were no trained scientists at the site before the eruption; it was only after news of an eruption got out that scientists would rush to the site. He argued that this was something that put the United States behind others.

It was this frustration that led Jaggar to leave MIT and establish the Hawaiian Volcano Observatory at Kilauea. Finally, the doctor had a site dedicated to the study and direct observation of volcanoes. Under his directorship, from 1912 to 1940, the Hawaiian Volcano Observatory became a pioneering part of fields vital to the study of volcanoes.

Jaggar felt Kilauea was perfect for a volcano observatory because it was the safest known volcano in the world, it was accessible (a day's sail from Honolulu and a 30-mile ride from Hilo's harbor), the climate was uniform, and the air was clear (for astronomy). Other contributing factors included the Central Pacific being a good location for recording distant earthquakes, the frequent small earthquakes that could be easily studied, the hot and cold underground waters available for study, and the site's presence in an United States territory. Additionally, Kilauea and Mauna Loa were isolated and free from certain complications that might skew data collected at other volcanic centers.

Jaggar and the scientists at the Hawaiian Volcano Observatory were not only able to learn how volcanoes worked, they were able to use seismograms to accurately predict the arrival of a tsunami created by distant earthquakes—this saved lives. For the first time, people living along the coastline of Hawaii could be successfully warned about when a tidal wave was coming.

Dr. Thomas Jaggar wanted the study of volcanoes to further science and help to reduce the loss of life and property that eruptions caused. Above, park superintendent Robert Barbee points out earthquake damage to Rosalynn and Amy Carter at Waldron Ledge on June 23, 1977. Below, the masonry walls at the Kalapana Ranch tumbled down during a 5.0 earthquake on June 30, 1997.

Dr. Thomas Jaggar insisted on getting access not only to the volcano at Kilauea, but also to the summit of Mauna Loa. Conditions were extreme, with violent winds, low temperatures, and rough lava on non-maintained trails. No water was available on site; it had to be carried in. Jaggar is credited with setting a trail from Hawaiian Volcano Observatory headquarters, at Kilauea, to the top of Mauna Loa. The trip to the top was so arduous and exhausting that overnight facilities were needed so that horses could rest and scientists would have time to conduct studies. Until the Hui O Pele group donated money for the building of the rest house at the Mauna Loa summit in 1934, hikers, riders, and scientists were forced to camp in Jaggar's Cave, a crack in the lava that had a corrugated metal sheet pulled over the top for a roof.

In a message delivered in 1941 and inserted into a cornerstone at Volcano House, Dr. Thomas A. Jaggar predicted that "the laboratories will be disseminated as underground earthquake-instrument cellars, underground temperature measuring wells, electrically controlled measurement stations reporting to a central office, and extended automatic and auto-metric facilities sending wired or wireless messages of underground and overground happenings on Mauna Loa. A volcano observatory must see or measure the whole volcano inside and out with all of science to help. The lesson of a third of a century has been to learn to look underground at the inner earth." Today, all of Dr. Jaggar's predictions have come true. Fifty-one seismic stations radio information to the Hawaiian Volcano Observatory, where an earthquake's epicenter is located by computer within minutes of it taking place. Thanks to these advances, scientists were able to gather more data from the pictured 1954 eruption at Halemaumau Crater than they had been a decade before.

A visitor stares into Halemaumau, the site of numerous volcanic eruptions. Dr. Thomas Jaggar chose to study volcanoes after being one of the few scientists from the United States to experience the devastating 1902 eruption in Martinique. In his autobiography, he wrote, "It was hard to distinguish where the streets had been. Everything was buried under fallen walls of cobblestone and pink plaster and tiles, including 20,000 bodies . . . As I look back on the Martinique experience I know what a crucial point in my life it was . . . I realized that the killing of thousands of persons by subterranean machinery totally unknown to geologists . . . was worthy of a life work."

After giving a lecture in Honolulu that focused on the Martinique expedition, Dr. Thomas Jaggar was approached by Lorrin A. Thurston, publisher of the *Pacific Commercial Advertiser*, about making the area around Kilauea into a scientific observatory. Within a year, Thurston and others raised the funds needed to begin the Hawaii Volcano Research Association. A small observation station was set up on the rim of Halemaumau Crater (pictured), and with additional support from Massachusetts Institute of Technology alumni, construction of the new Hawaiian Volcano Observatory started in 1912 in the cellar of the Volcano House hotel.

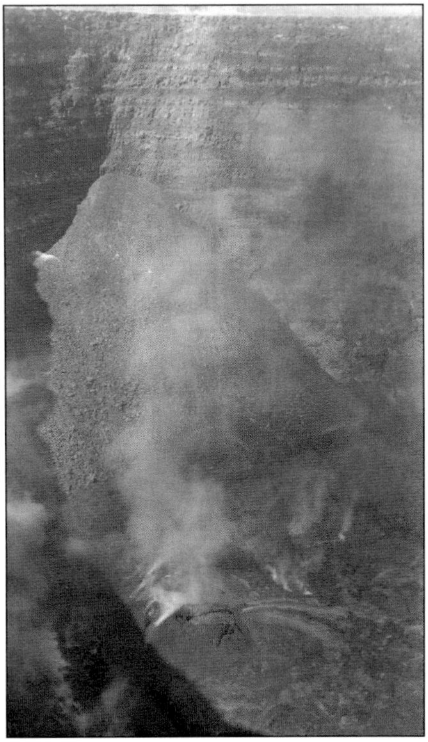

This fuming cone—part of the 1930 Halemaumau eruption—was one of the reasons that Dr. Thomas Jaggar wanted to have an on-site observation operation at an active volcano. During his early years as director of the Hawaiian Volcano Observatory, Jaggar struggled to get adequate funding. In 1919, Jaggar finally got federal funding from the National Weather Service. Then, in 1924, the United States Geological Survey took over the operation of the observatory. They have retained control of the observatory since except for a brief period during the Depression when the National Park Service took over.

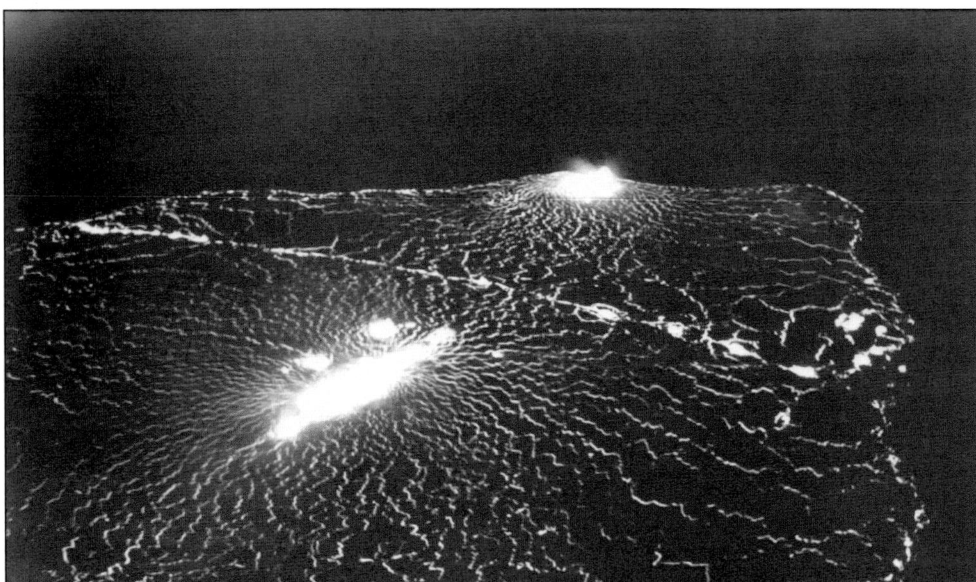

The eruption and lava lake from the 1930 Halemaumau eruption was monitored by the Hawaiian Volcano Observatory, just as Dr. Thomas Jaggar hoped. Today, electronic equipment monitors earthquakes from several sites within Hawai'i Volcanoes National Park, and this information is immediately uploaded to the internet. Live camera feeds also broadcast footage of the eruptions. Residents of Hawaii have become reliant on the Hawaiian Volcano Observatory's monitoring of sulfur emissions (locally known as "vog"). If these dangerous emissions reach high levels, the observatory sends out alerts that may result in having to close certain areas within the park.

This September 6, 1934, photograph shows lava cascading from the southeast side of Halemaumau Crater. This was the first day of an eruption that lasted 33 days; Dr. Thomas Jaggar's Hawaiian Volcano Observatory recorded rockslides in Halemaumau Crater, a southwesterly tilt of Kilauea's summit, and several earthquakes.

This September 11, 1934, photograph shows lava fountains rising up from three points in Halemaumau Crater. These fountains, which were located along the western wall of the crater, sprayed lava up to 900 feet in height. The lava flowed across the crater floor, creating a lake that reached depths of 60 feet in only a few hours. In a radio broadcast from the rim of Halemaumau Crater, Dr. Thomas Jaggar told a national audience that the eruption was "indescribably beautiful." After the broadcast, more and more visitors clamored to see the eruption.

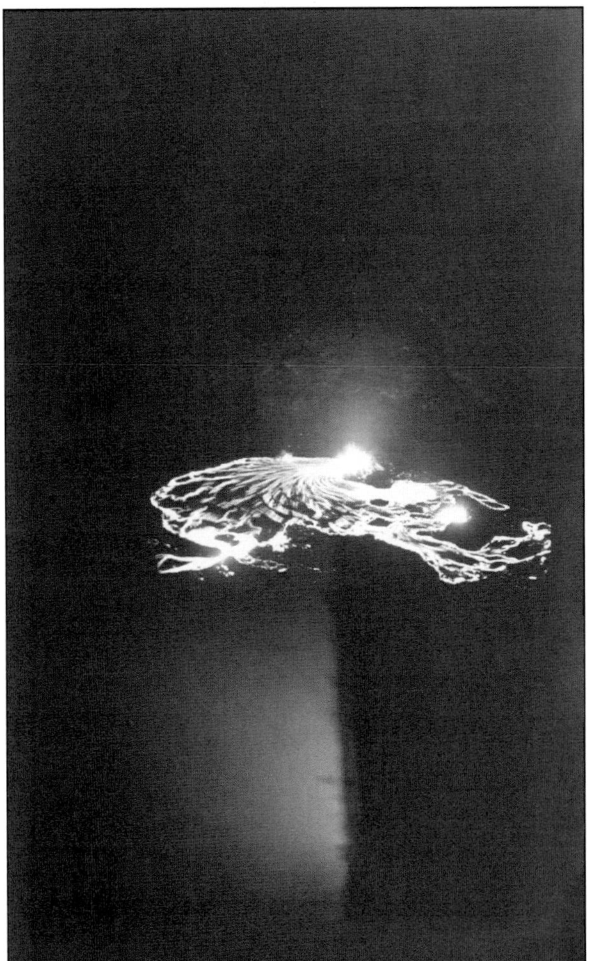

In the first 12 hours of the 1934 eruption, the volcano produced fountains of lava, ferocious rumbling noises, earthquakes, and the release of hot gases into the air. The eruption created whirling winds of pumice and dust and filled the air with the smell of sulfur dioxide.

On September 21, 1934—just over two weeks into the eruption—the west and northwest fountain eruptions had stopped, but the north fountains continued to blow at the center of the lava lake.

The dramatic 1934 eruption had everything—spurting lava fountains, red molten lava pouring through cracks in the crater wall and floor, and violent outbursts of gas from the drained lava lake, which people could hear from as far away as three miles.

The fountains of the 1934 eruption finally ceased on October 8, 33 days after the eruption began. After the dramatic geological episodes that accompanied this eruption—lava fountains, earthquakes, blasts of gas, and hails of pumice—Kilauea was quiet for the next 18 years. This was the longest period of inactivity in the volcano's recorded history.

After 18 years, on June 27, 1952, Kilauea erupted again, sending fountains of lava across the crater floor. The Hawaiian Volcano Observatory reported that during this eruption, rocks (some measuring four inches across) rained down on the surrounding area.

During the 1952 eruption, the lava fountains regularly reached 100 feet in height, occasionally jumping into the 400- to 800-foot range along the southwest wall of the crater. The accumulated lava on the floor of the crater buried the older splatter cones.

A section of the Halemaumau Crater's wall collapsed during the 1952 eruption. Due to heavy fumes, visibility was poor, and the reason for the collapse is not known. On November 10, 1952, after 136 days, the last lava fountain ceased, and the eruption was over.

Four

Hawaiian Culture Today

The plaintive wailing of the conch shell rises through the spidery mist of Halemaumau Crater, heralding the beginning of the Big Island's annual Aloha Festivals. A chanter cries out in the native Hawaiian tongue that a new king is to be crowned. This is done as part of the *Ka Ho'ola'a Ana* (investiture), which traditionally marks the beginning of the month-long events of the Aloha Festivals celebrated throughout the islands.

Tradition sets the tone during this reenactment of the Hawaiian ceremony to crown a new *Mo'i* (king). As in old Hawaii, the event is held at high noon, when the sun is at its zenith. Ancient tradition believes that the strength of the Hawaiian gods is transferred into the king when the sun's rays strike the top of the new leader's head.

The Aloha Festivals are the largest celebration of Hawaiian culture in the United States. Originally created as Aloha Week by the Jaycees civic group in 1946, the festival honored Hawaii's music, dance, and history as a way of perpetuating the unique cultural traditions of the islands. The statewide celebrations became the Aloha Festivals in 1991. More than 100,000 residents and visitors across the state attend the festivities each year.

The festivals begin with a volunteer royal court being taken to the edge of the Halemaumau Crater on the top of Kilauea. There, the outgoing court is thanked for their services to the island people, and the incoming *Mo'i* and *Mo'i Wahine* (queen) are elevated to their positions. The king is draped with a feather cloak and tall helmet, denoting his rank, and the queen has a necklace of her rank tied around her neck.

Ho'okupu (gifts of the land) are given to Pele because she is revered as "Mother Earth." The volcano goddess is given the honor and glory of "giving birth" to new land, and the new royal court asks for her blessings as they celebrate her name in chant and hula.

To be chosen to serve in the Aloha Festivals' royal court is an honor. Candidates are screened for their Hawaiian bloodlines, genealogy, and dedication to Hawaiian culture and heritage.

Following the investiture, the festival continues with arts and crafts, demonstrations, and other cultural events held at the Volcano Arts Center in the park.

The Aloha Festivals represent just one of the myriad ways that ancient Hawaiian culture is still celebrated today.

This January 3, 1932, eruption of Halemaumau—along with other awe-inspiring eruptions—continues to drive the Hawaiian people as they keep their culture and traditions alive. Hawaii has had two cultural renaissances, with the first beginning under King David Kalakaua in 1874. The second began in the 1970s, when there was a widespread surge of interest in Hawaiian music, dance, language, and cultural practices.

The kingdom of Hawaii, although officially Christian, still had numerous believers in the power of the Hawaiian volcano goddess, Pele—especially an angry Pele. They frequently pointed to movement inside the crater—such as the rockslide pictured above—as proof of her displeasure. When King Kamehameha V died on December 12, 1872, without a successor to the throne, the kingdom was thrown into turmoil. Under the new Kingdom of Hawaii's constitution, if a king died without naming a successor, the Hawaii legislature would appoint a king. In 1873, Hawaii's king was selected by an elected legislative body for the first time.

Visitors watch during the annual reenactment ceremony to crown a king on the rim of a crater in Hawai'i Volcanoes National Park. The new royal court (at left side in the image, with standard bearers holding the *kahili*, or feathered stand, which shows that royalty is present) faces hula dancers (sitting on *lauhala* mats) and the public to begin the investiture. In 1872, when Hawaii was without a king, it was up to the legislature to appoint a new king. There were several candidates for the Hawaiian throne, but the contest centered on two high-ranking *alii* (chiefs): William C. Lunalilo and David Kalakaua. Lunalilo was more popular—partially because he was a higher-ranking chief than Kalakaua—and was the immediate cousin of the previous king, Kamehameha V. Lunalilo was also the more liberal of the two, and he promised to amend the constitution to give the people a greater voice in their government.

The same hula and chants performed when a new king was crowned are still practiced today during the annual Aloha Festivals. Here, the new royal court, in the stands on risers (note the king and his feathered helmet), watches hula dancers perform the same dances and chants that were performed in ancient Hawaii for centuries during the investiture of a new king. Before Kamehameha V's death left Hawaii without a king in 1872, Hawaiians had lived for generations with one king following another. They felt that the government should simply declare Lunalilo as the king. Lunalilo, however, refused this, insisting that everyone in the kingdom should take part in an election.

Hula dancers (on *lauhala* mat) face the new king (on riser) and chant ancient songs that date back thousands of years and ask the gods to bless and guide the new king. In 1872, when David Kalakaua was running for King of Hawaii, he was considered to be the conservative candidate over his opponent, William C. Lunalilo. At the time, foreigners dominated the Hawaiian government, and Kalakaua promised to put native Hawaiians back into the kingdom's government. He also promised to amend the kingdom's constitution. On January 1, 1873, an election was held for the office of King of Hawaii. Lunalilo won by an overwhelming majority, and the next day, the legislature confirmed the popular vote by unanimously electing Lunalilo. Kalakaua then conceded.

Here, visitors watch the annual reenactment of the investiture of the king during the annual Aloha Festivals on the rim of the crater. The procession of the royal court is leaving the investiture headed by the standard bearers holding the *kahili*, which indicates that royalty is present. In ancient Hawaii, commoners fell on their knees or lay prostrate whenever royalty was present. Although William C. Lunalilo won the popular vote and was elected by the Hawaiian legislature in 1873, he died just over a year later on February 3, 1874. David Kalakaua was then selected by the legislature to succeed him.

The reenactment of the investiture of the king (pictured) is just one of the ways that Hawaiian culture is practiced today. King David Kalakaua was nicknamed the "Merrie Monarch" by King Charles II of England due to the Hawaiian's love of fun. He also is recognized for resurrecting traditional Hawaiian culture. During his reign, hula was revived; the dance had been banned by Queen Kaahumanu in 1830 after she converted to Christianity. Today, Kalakaua's name lives on in the Merrie Monarch Festival, an annual hula festival named in his honor. He is also known for reviving surfing, as well as the Hawaiian martial art known as Lua. He and his brother and sisters were known as the "Royal Fours" for their musical talents, and he wrote "Hawai'i Pono'ī," which is the state song of Hawaii. King Kalakaua's support of the ukulele, which first arrived on the islands during his reign, led to it becoming a symbol of Hawaii and Hawaiian culture.

In the annual reenactment of the ceremony to crown a king, volunteers dress in traditional garb. The procession is led by the conch blower, followed by the tall *ihe* (spear) carrier and *kahili* (feathered stand) carrier. All three of these figures announce that an *alii* (high chief) is coming. In ancient Hawaii, commoners fell to their knees or laid flat on the ground to show their respect. During the ceremony, the king wears the feathered cloak and tall helmet that denote his rank, while the queen wears a necklace that represents hers.

The above photograph shows the opening of a traditional *imu* (pit oven). The star of most luau is the pig, which is placed in an imu, cooked for several hours, then uncovered and removed as the luau begins. The hot coals are removed once the food is cooked, and the meat is then removed and shredded. This allows the melted fat to mix with the meat, maintaining a uniform consistency and flavor. The second Hawaiian renaissance occurred in the 1970s. Hawaiian music became popular in this period, and there was a resurgence of people learning the Hawaiian language (Hawaiian immersion schools were opened at this time), hula, traditional Hawaiian crafts (like weaving *lahala*), and Hawaiian studies.

At 5:53 p.m., on September 20, 1934, Pele began another eruption in Halemaumau—drawing people to the Big Island to experience a volcanic eruption.

The ancient art of hula, banned by Queen Kaahumanu in 1830 after she converted to Christianity, is very much alive today. Hula may appear to only be a dance, but it also portrays a chant or song via the accompanying hand and arm motions. Generally, hula is divided into two categories—*auana* and *kahiko*. The ancient hula performed before Westerners arrived in Hawaii is called *kahiko* and is generally accompanied by a chant and traditional Hawaiian instruments. The dance performed after Westerners arrived is called *auana* (to wander), and this type of hula can be accompanied by song and instruments like the guitar or ukulele. Hula is taught in a school known as a *halau* and taught by a teacher called a *kumu hula* (kumu means "source of knowledge").

Here, hula is performed for the royal court during the annual Aloha Festivals at Hawai'i Volcanoes National Park. Numerous legends point to the origin of hula. One tells the story of Laka, the goddess of hula, who gave birth to the dance on the island of Molokai (Molokai residents still celebrate this at the Ka Hula Piko festival, which is held each May). Another legend talks of Hiiaka, a sister of Pele, and says that hula originated on the Big Island. Yet another legend tells that Pele was running away from her sister Namakaokahai, goddess of the oceans, when she found an island where she could not be touched by waves (the Big Island), and she danced the first hula in celebration of her victory over the ocean.

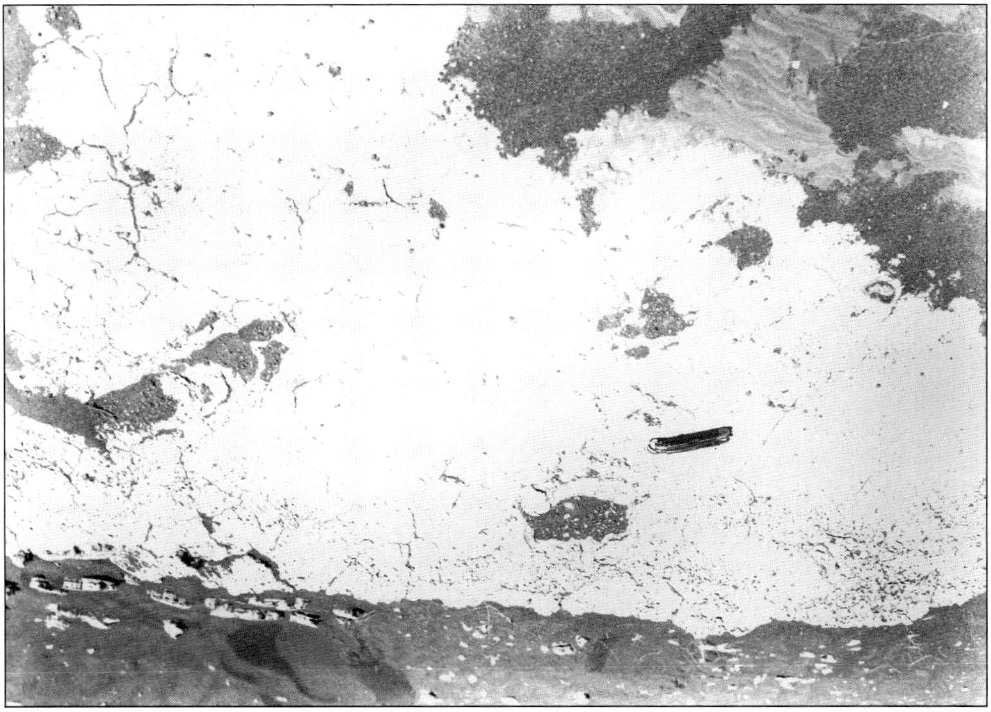

The above image shows footprints in the volcanic ash, and below is the park's Footprints Interpretive Shelter. The footprints, which are listed in the National Register of Historic Places, are an unusual feature found nowhere else in Hawaii. In 1782, Kalaniopuu, a high chief of Hawaii, died after naming his son, Kiwalao, as the new high chief. Kalaniopuu's nephew, Kamehameha (who later became a great chief who united the Hawaiian islands), had hoped to be named as successor. Upset that he had not been named high chief, Kamehameha decided to overthrow his cousin. In July 1782, after a lengthy battle, some of Kiwalao's family members escaped. Keoua, Kiwalao's half-brother, headed back to his home in Kau, but the route he and his army took brought them to Kilauea, where Pele was in the midst of a fiery eruption. Keoua decided to stay in Kilauea, and he split his army into three different companies that left the crater at different times. One company had just left when the earth shook; volcanic ash and hot gas exploded out of the crater, and a dense cloud of ash, sand, and rocks rained down. A second company came upon the first and found them all face down in the ash. People speculated that the footprints in the ash were left by these warriors, but recent archeological and geological research indicates that the footprints may not be from the eruption but rather evidence of everyday activities in the area.

Visitors from around the globe sign up for the free interpretive talks given at Halemaumau, where they learn about Hawaiian culture and eruptions like the one below, which was photographed in 1952. This eruption began 20 minutes before midnight on June 27 and continued for 136 days.

The Queen's Bath, located near Kaimu Beach in Kalapana, is now buried under 30 to 75 feet of lava. The spring-fed pool was a collapsed lava tube that filled with fresh water from natural springs. In ancient Hawaii, only the *alii* (chiefs) were allowed in these waters, which were considered sacred. Starting with the 1983 Kilauea eruption, lava started flowing downhill toward the fishing village of Kalapana. As the flow grew closer, it moved to the west, avoiding the town and Queen's Bath. When Kilauea erupted again in 1990, spewing out lava from April to December, the lava flow swallowed almost the entire town. As it rolled over houses, stores, and churches, the slow-moving lava gave the residents time to leave. Today, the area is a ghost town buried under shiny black pahoehoe lava, but there are still a few residents who access their homes via four-wheel-drive vehicles and live without access to water or electricity.

Before the 1990 eruption buried the town of Kalapana in lava, churches (like the one pictured) dotted the landscape. The most famous church in Kalapana was the Star of the Sea Painted Church, which was built in 1927–1928. It was constructed under the direction of the Belgian Catholic missionary Fr. Evarist Gielen, who painted the upper section of the church's interior. The paintings tell the story of Father Damien (now St. Damien) of Molokai and his work with sufferers of leprosy. The wooden Roman Catholic church (pictured at its Kalapana location) was moved just an hour before the lava flow reached the point where it had sat for 62 years. Just a week before, the congregation had decided to save the church, which is listed in the National Register of Historic Places because of the hand-painted murals on the walls and ceiling. Moving the painted church involved lifting it onto a flatbed truck while a crew cleared the road ahead of hanging utility lines and tree branches. Star of the Sea now sits on Highway 130 between mile markers 19 and 20.

Just one year after the spectacular 1959–1960 eruptions, Kilauea resumed erupting at 4 a.m. on February 24, 1961. A small, shallow earthquake struck and then continued for the next seven months. During the eruption, 18.2 million cubic yards of lava flowed from the summit.

By 7:00 a.m., on February 24, 1961, a volcanic fume started rising from Halemaumau Crater that could be seen from the eastern rim. The eruption came from the northeast pit in the crater floor, where a lava fountain was spurting 50 to 100 feet high as a series of smaller fountains were also active. By 8:10 a.m., two additional vents were erupting.

When word spreads that Kilauea is erupting, people flock from around the globe to the volcano. These nuns, fighting the mountain winds, are making their way along the Devastation Trail at Hawai'i Volcanoes National Park. This trail, which is accessible for wheelchairs and strollers, is an easy, one-mile boardwalk loop through the cinder outfall of the 1959 Kilauea Iki eruption.

The Iliahi (Sandalwood) Trail is a popular, moderately difficult 1.5-mile loop that begins and ends next to Volcano House, sends visitors through a Hawaiian rainforest, and passes by steam vents and earth cracks left by past eruptions.

Just before midnight on June 27, 1952, John Forbes—a scientist at Hawaiian Volcano Observatory—reported a fountain eruption at Halemaumau. Within minutes, a thick, sulfurous fume cloud had moved in and tephra (rocks, ash, gases, and other materials from a volcanic eruption) began to rain down upon the earth.

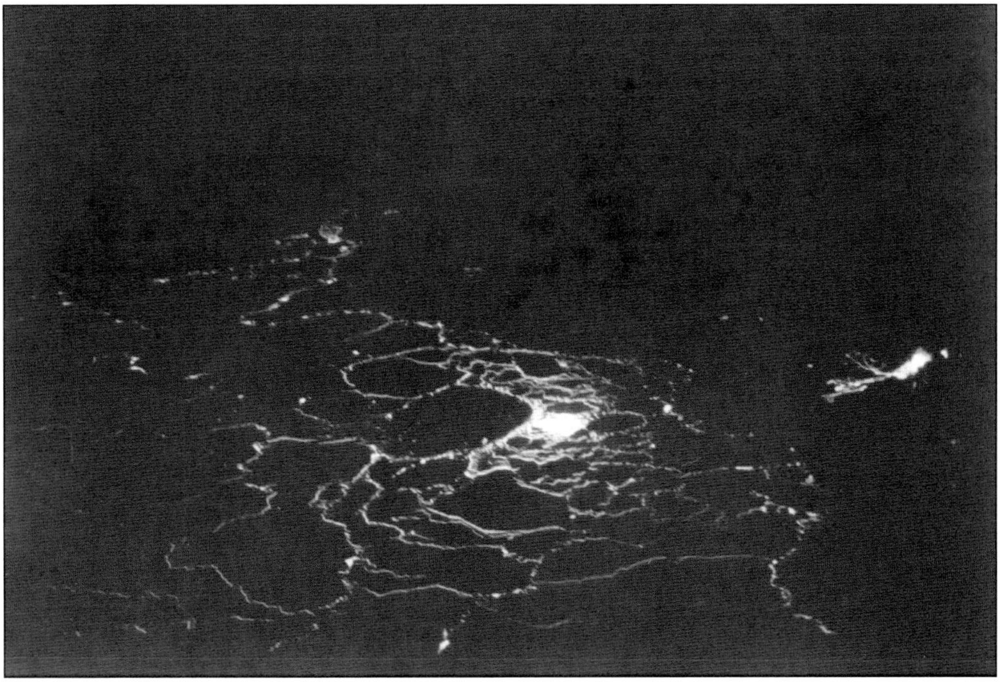

The 1952 eruption at Halemaumau quickly expanded into a near-continuous line of lava fountains reaching 2,500 feet in length, crossing the crater floor from the southwest to the northeast edges, and extending partway up the crater wall.

During the 1952 eruption, individual fountains roared up 50 to 100 feet, with an occasional fountain jetting up to 400 or 800 feet. Views of this spectacular eruption were intermittent due to heavy fume clouds, but scientists quickly noted that the older spatter cones on the crater floor had already been buried beneath the rising lava lake. This suggested that more than 4 million cubic yards of lava emerged in the first 30 minutes of the eruption.

After a series of earthquakes in the last two weeks of June 1961, the eruption moved into its third and final phase. The number of daily earthquakes went from 175 to 100, though only a few could be felt by the general public. At 8:00 p.m., on July 10, 1961, tall lava fountains could be seen along the central and southwest crater floor. The height of the main fountain reached 600 feet as pumice fell on the rim of Halemaumau.

Just a couple of hours after midnight on November 5, 1967, a dozen fountains of lava lit up the night sky with showers of red molten rock shooting some 200 to 250 feet in the air. Pele had erupted again from the floor of the Halemaumau Crater. The spectacular eruption left an orange glow in the sky, which people in Hilo, 30 miles away, reported seeing. Just as suddenly as the eruption had begun, it stopped just 22.5 hours later. The only remaining evidence of the dramatic eruption was the "bathtub ring" on the side of the light-colored rocks resulting from the quickly swollen, then drained, lava lake. The "ring" can still be seen today.

Five

Mauna Loa, the Sleeping Giant, Awakens

Mauna Loa (Long Mountain) is one of the Earth's largest and most active volcanoes. Since 1843, Mauna Loa has erupted 33 times, with eruptions lasting from 1 to 145 days. The lava from the last eruption, in 1984, came within four and a half miles of Hilo, the island's capital.

A missionary made the first written record of a Mauna Loa eruption in June 1832. He watched the eruption from the island of Maui, some 118 miles away.

Other dramatic eruptions include the 1855–1856 eruption, which produced the largest volume of lava seen by modern observers. The 1868 eruption caused the largest earthquake in Hawaii's history—it measured 8.0 on the Richter scale.

The 1950 eruption, which lasted from June 1 to June 13, began with a curtain of lava spreading along a 12-mile fissure. Within 4 hours, floods of lava poured from the vents, and a cloud of fumes rose two miles into the sky.

The 1984 eruption, which formally lasted from March 24 to April 15, actually began when a series of earthquakes began to steadily increase in frequency in mid-September 1983. By March 24, 1984, small earthquakes were occurring every two to three minutes. Finally, at 1:00 a.m. on March 25, the earthquakes became so fierce that the telescopes on Mauna Kea, 26 miles away, could not be stabilized due to the constant vibration. At 1:25 a.m., a military satellite recorded the infrared glow signaling an eruption at the summit. By 7:00 a.m., fissures were spurting lava. Finally, by 9:30 a.m., a curtain of fire that was 1.2 miles long had erupted, with fountains of lava reaching between 32 and 164 feet in height.

On the first day, lava had rolled five and a half miles downhill and was threatening Kulani Prison. The lava then diverted around the prison and continued down the steep terrain toward Hilo.

Choking smoke from burning vegetation filled the air, booming explosions from the methane gas shattered the peaceful surroundings, and intense light from the flowing red lava lit the night sky. People in Hilo were very nervous.

Suddenly, the lava flow stagnated. The output at the source slowed, and the lava became more viscous, which resulted in the channels of the flow blocking up and slowing down. The lava had stopped just four and a half miles from the island's population center.

Mauna Loa, the world's largest volcano, rises 13,678 feet above sea level. Due to the mountain's incredible volume, the seafloor has become depressed, and the summit sits 56,000 feet above the seabed. This sloping shield volcano covers an area of 2,035 square miles—half of the island of Hawaii.

The 1949 eruption began with a fountain of lava streaming from a fissure on the slope. Most of Mauna Loa's eruptions come from fissures that are on either the northeast or southwest rift zones. The cloud of steam rising over the fiery lava extended two miles into the air and could be seen from a great distance.

This volcanic cone, created during the 134-day eruption in 1940, shows the jagged remains of the 1949 fissure, which exploded with lava. Mauna Loa first erupted on the sea floor between 700,000 and 1 million years ago, finally rising from the ocean as an island some 400,000 years ago.

In this image, lava pours out of Mauna Loa. In the 33 eruptions of the volcano since 1843, the lava produced has covered 310 square miles of land on the island of Hawaii. One eruption on the southwest rift zone traveled the nine miles to the ocean in less than three hours. The land where the city of Hilo now stands was covered by lava from Mauna Loa during a 1880–1881 eruption.

The isolated (and difficult to reach) Mauna Kea is shown in this photograph as clouds roll in beneath the summit. It was not until 1984 that scientists were able to study the volcano's eruptions up close, as steep terrain had prevented close inspection during the 1950 eruption, and scientists were forced to make observations from the highway. Unfortunately, helicopters were not available at that time.

Fountains of lava explode from the Moku'aweoweo Caldera, which measures nearly two miles by three miles and is 600 feet deep. These summit depressions generally form over a shallow subsurface reservoir or magma changer. Depending on the size of the depression, it is either called a caldera (if its diameter is more than one mile) or a crater (if its diameter is smaller than one mile).

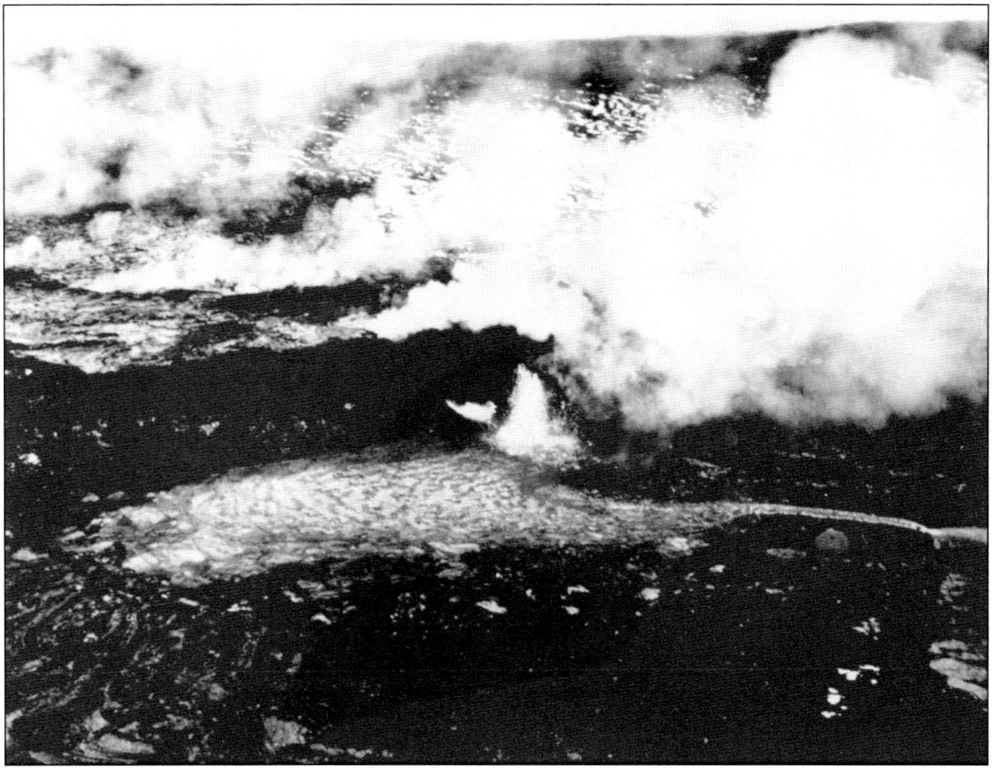

A fountain of lava gushes along the south wall of the Moku'aweoweo Caldera in this photograph taken at the beginning of the 1949 eruption, which lasted for 145 days. On the afternoon of January 6, 1949, scientists at the Hawaiian Volcano Observatory—just 20 miles away from the summit of Mauna Loa—could not see the mountain, as it was shrouded in heavy cloud cover. They could, however, hear the deep rumble from the summit that signaled an eruption.

The January 6, 1949, eruption began with a series of three-mile-long fissures along the southwest floor of Mauna Loa's summit caldera. Lava fountains shot 100 feet into the air, gushing along the entire three miles. Within 24 hours of the eruption's beginning, most of the southern half of the caldera's floor was buried under pahoehoe (smooth) lava, leaving the 1940 cone sticking out like an island in a sea of molten lava.

After emerging during the 1949 summit eruption, these rivers of lava raced down the mountain at a rate of about six miles per day, causing the short-lived—but frightening—evacuation of Honaunau residents on January 7. With knowledge about the potential dangers presented by active volcanoes and the incredibly destructive powers of lava, Big Island residents are mindful of warnings from the County of Hawaii Civil Defense Agency and the Hawaiian Volcano Observatory.

By January 9, 1949, the eruption was centered on two lava fountains located at the southwest edge of Moku'aweoaweo Caldera. Over the next two weeks, the fountains of lava grew stronger, reaching heights of more than 500 feet on January 23 with occasional bursts of up to 800 feet. Notice the pahoehoe lava spreading out across the crater floor.

Lava flowing from the summit crater cascaded into the South Pit, a crater adjoining the south side of the caldera. Lava gradually filled the South Pit until it overflowed on January 25, spilling out to the southeast. This flow advanced almost five and a half miles down the volcano's flank, to Wood Valley, before stalling on January 31.

An aerial view of the summit—such as this one, which shows the 1940 cinder cone surrounded by lava—was highly sought during the eruption. Despite harsh winter conditions and the difficulty of reaching the 13,680-foot elevation, people flocked to Hawaii Island to get a glimpse of Pele's latest eruption. Swarms of planes circled the summit, hundreds of cars jammed the two-lane highway to the summit, and a special steamer excursion from Honolulu promised that passengers would get to see views of the eruption from the sea.

Outside of the Moku'aweoweo Caldera, steam from fissures filled the air, and lava flows rolled down the flanks of Mauna Loa. Due to the difficulty of studying the volcano, scientists are not sure of the exact date when the 1949 eruption ended. Volcanologists estimate that it lasted between 145 and 147 days, making it second only to the 560-day eruption of Mauna Loa in 1873–1874.

This dramatic red fountain of fire from the 1949 eruption began to slow down and weaken in February. As the shooting fountains decreased in size, the eruption began to spit out a denser form of lava. On February 5, the fountain of lava briefly settled before restarting and continuing until June 1.

Fountains of lava reached as high as 600 feet during the largest and most spectacular eruption recorded at the southwest rift zone of Mauna Kea, in 1950. Lava poured out of a nearly continuous 12.4-mile long fissure, and the plume clouds hovering above the fountains told scientists that the activity was migrating down the rift. In less than four hours, the lava had reached the ocean on the western side of the island.

The 1950 eruption of Mauna Loa lasted for 23 days and produced 376 million cubic meters of lava—the largest recorded outpouring of lava from the southwest rift zone of the mountain. In this photograph, a boulder the size of a two-story house moves swiftly down the slope.

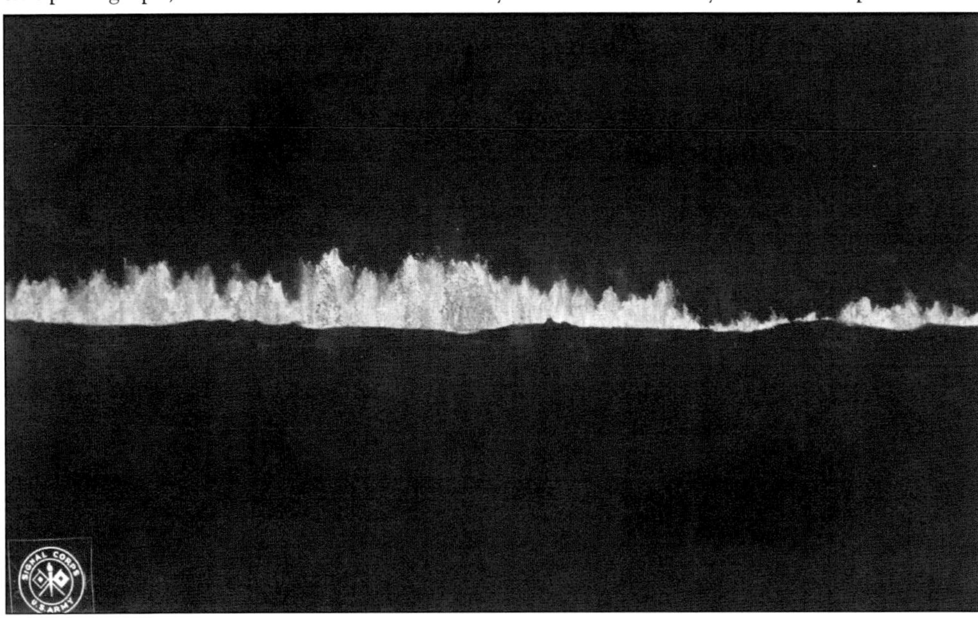

This aerial photograph of the 1950 eruption was taken by a plane flying just below the top of the 600-foot tall fountains of fire. Magma pressure in Mauna Loa remained high after the 1949 eruption, producing—in a relatively short period—the highest amount of lava that has ever been recorded.

Due to the steep terrain and the sheer volume of lava, the 1950 eruption at Mauna Loa's southwest rift zone moved quickly down the slopes of the mountain. Scientists from the Hawaiian Volcano Observatory estimated the velocity of the lava flow at 10 to 30 miles per hour. The lava reached the ocean in record time.

The numerous flows of the 1950 Mauna Loa eruption could be seen from the water. The first flow made the 15-mile journey to the ocean in less than three hours. The cloud of steam, which is rising a half-mile into the air, demonstrates the cooling effect that water has on lava.

This aerial photograph of the 1950 eruption shows ribbons of lava snaking down the mountain and exploding into the ocean. Scientists generally expect more of an explosion when 1,200- to 2,000-degree Fahrenheit lava hits 70-degree ocean water, but in this case, the explosion was minor.

Rivers of molten lava roll down the flanks of Mauna Loa in this photograph of the 1950 eruption. Depending on its temperature, lava ranges in color from brownish red (temperature ranging from 932 to 1,202 degrees Fahrenheit) to red (1,202 to 1,472 degrees Fahrenheit) to dark red (1,472 to 1,832 degrees Fahrenheit) to vivid orange (above 1,832 degrees Fahrenheit).

In this photograph, lava from the western flank of the 1950 Mauna Loa eruption floods down the mountain and shoots into the ocean. Note the rising plume of steam, half a mile out to sea, marking the submarine front of the flow. When lava meets the ocean, it vaporizes seawater and creates a dense plume of steam. Over time, the lava builds a delta that extends the shoreline of the island.

This photograph from the 1950 Mauna Loa eruption shows Pele at work, building more land. After lava flows into the ocean, it begins to cling to the rocky shoreline and slowly spreads out to sea in fan-shaped platforms known as a lava delta. Lava pours into the ocean from either surface flows or from lava tubes below the water. This underwater lava tends to cools rapidly. As the lava cools, scientists describe the breakdown of this hot, molten lava as shattering into "sand-like" fragments. As more and more lava continues to flow into the ocean, these fragments slowly build up and eventually form a foundation. Over time, the foundation grows, and an entirely new parcel of land is added along the shoreline.

This aerial photograph of the 1950 Mauna Loa eruption shows lava pouring into the ocean at two locations—one large flow at left and a smaller one at right. The river of lava is clearly visible in the background, and steam rises in the foreground as the hot lava hits the cool waters of the Pacific Ocean.

For 23 days, lava from the 1950 eruption flowed from the summit of Mauna Loa and down the steep side of the mountain. After crossing the slopes, it plunged over the 50- to 80-foot-high *pali* (cliffs) on its way to the ocean. Many fish were killed when the lava reached the sea, including many unidentified deep-water species.

This aerial photograph of lava pouring into the ocean shows the volume of lava produced during the 1950 Mauna Loa eruption. Scientists estimate that the lava that remained above sea level measured approximately 387 million cubic meters. The amount that entered the sea was more difficult to determine, but it is estimated to have exceeded 76 million cubic meters. The total volume of lava erupted totaled at least 460 million cubic meters.

In the early morning of July 6, 1975, lava erupted from fissures high on the northeast rift zone of Mauna Loa and shot fountains of fire into the air. These fissures fed several lava flows, the longest of which traveled three miles toward Mauna Kea, located 26 miles north.

Due to heavy rainfall in early 1975, there still was snow atop both Mauna Loa and Mauna Kea in July. This painting illustrates a spectacular fountain of lava alongside snow still on the mountain during the 1975 eruption on Mauna Loa.

Despite the dramatic curtain of fire in the background of this painting and the large field of pahoehoe lava in the foreground, the 1975 eruption lasted for less than one day. Although the eruption ended before nightfall, elevated earthquake activity continued for another six days as magma moved into the northeast rift zone without reaching the surface. As long as magma threatened to erupt again, the scientists at Hawaiian Volcano Observatory continued to monitor the volcano around the clock.

Six

Kilauea, Hawaii's Most Active Volcano

At the flank of Mauna Loa is Kilauea, the youngest volcano in the Hawaiian Islands. Scientists estimate that the 4,091-foot-tall Kilauea began forming on the ocean floor between 300,000 and 600,000 years ago and appeared above sea level between 50,000 and 100,000 years ago.

Throughout its history, Kilauea has been very active. Though the majority of these eruptions are relatively gentle, with fountains of lava spouting into the air and then rolling down the steep terrain, the volcano has produced powerful explosions on occasion. Some have thrown huge boulders—as large as a two-story house and weighing several tons—into the air. The 1790 eruption was particularly lethal, killing several warriors as they fought in a battle between competing groups of Hawaiians.

Another lethal explosion occurred in 1924. Ruy Finch, director of the Hawaiian Volcanoes Observatory at the time, described the eruption as "large puffs of steam" and "numerous earthquakes and rumbling" with a "wave of increased air pressure" that came before boulders began to rain down from the crater. Additionally, Lorrin Thurston, publisher of the *Honolulu Advertiser*, wrote, "the sand blown out [of the crater] was so hot that it scorched green vegetation more than 3,000 feet from the pit. The rocks shot out are also white-hot."

Although not as explosive, the 36-day Kilauea eruption in 1960 threatened the small downslope villages of Kao'e and Kapoho before the lava entered the ocean. The two towns were left virtually intact, though they sustained minimal lava damage, and a blanket of lava, pumice, and ash covered the areas.

From 1983 to 1990, lava from Kilauea covered the communities on the south coast of the Big Island, destroying more than 180 homes, a Hawai'i Volcanoes National Park visitor's center, highways, and a number of historical and archeological sites. The lava also flowed into the small Kalapana community, burning homes and demolishing parks, roads, and gardens.

The eruption that began on January 3, 1983, continues at the time of writing (in late 2014). It is not only the longest recorded eruption to date in Hawaii or the United States—it is the longest recorded eruption in the entire world.

The scientists at the Hawaiian Volcano Observatory believe that the lava pond from the 1923 Halemaumau eruption drained down the rift zone and into the Kapoho area, which then resulted in earthquakes, ground faults, and 1924's rare, "explosive" eruption. Halemaumau Crater was 377 feet deep in the above 1923 photograph, and the lava lake drained and filled repeatedly. On April 29, 1924, the floor of the lake collapsed following an earthquake located downslope in Puna. Viewing conditions became horrible as rocks began falling into the lake and creating pillars of smoke. The falling rocks built up on the sinking floor, and the lava continued to build. On May 1, the floor was 492 feet deep, and by May 7, it was 688 feet deep.

The 1924 Kilauea eruption began on May 13. Oliver Emerson, a research fellow for the Hawaiian Volcano Research Association, wrote that at "about 9 (am) [the weather] became clear, showing volume of smoke rising from pit increased further . . . Cloud rose to height of 7,500 feet more or less above pit, and whole sky to south of pit deep purple, almost black. During morning thunder of avalanches plainly audible on bluff in front of (Kilauea) Military Camp." Emerson, wearing a gas mask, braved the eruption to explore the Halemaumau area and reported that explosions of rocks thrown out of Halemaumau were landing 600 to 800 feet away. Most of the rocks were small, but a few weighed 200 pounds. He stayed all night at the crater, reporting earthquakes and "considerable steam rising from the north side of pit."

In this photograph taken during the 1924 eruption at Halemaumau, Dr. R.J. Baker stands behind a 14-ton boulder that was thrown from the crater during a steam explosion. W.O. Clark, a geologist working for a local sugar company (he had previously worked for the United States Geological Survey) ventured to the park to watch the eruption and noted that "the majority of rocks, judging from their position and bounce mark, came down nearly vertical, though some showed horizontal component." Explosive eruptions are very unusual for Kilauea and occur about once per century. Several people were killed—mostly by falling boulders—during the 1924 eruption.

At approximately 8:30 a.m., on May 22, 1924, an explosion inside Halemaumau created the pictured fume cloud. As visitors to the park watched from Volcano House, the cloud quickly rose to an estimated two and a half miles in height. Observers said that they saw three lightning bolts inside the cloud. Note the dust that was kicked up by rocks showering down on the caldera floor.

In 1924, due to continued violent eruptions, Thomas Boles—then superintendent of the Hawai'i Volcanoes National Park—ordered the closure of the park. The *Honolulu Advertiser* reported, "The air about the volcano is highly charged with static electricity. Fuses at the Volcano House have been blown out and telephone communication is spasmodic . . . all foliage within two miles of the Volcano is covered with ashes and pierced with pebbles. Mud stands an inch thick on the porch of Boles' house, and has hardened to the consistency of cement. The eave gutters of the Volcano House are broken by the weight of the ashes and pebbles. Angleworms are lying dead all about the area."

This photograph of a dust cloud rising over the crater was taken from the park superintendent's house on February 20, 1928. Since there was no active eruption at the time, park personnel guessed that the dust was most likely the result of falling rocks or a landslide.

The 1930 rockslide inside Halemaumau Crater contributed to the building of the crater as it exists today. Rockslides were frequently precipitated by an earthquake, were extremely loud (some people thought they were explosions), and left dust lingering in the air for hours.

This photograph, taken at 5 a.m. on December 23, 1931, shows the fountain and lava lake produced by that year's eruption of Halemaumau. This particular eruption lasted for 14 days.

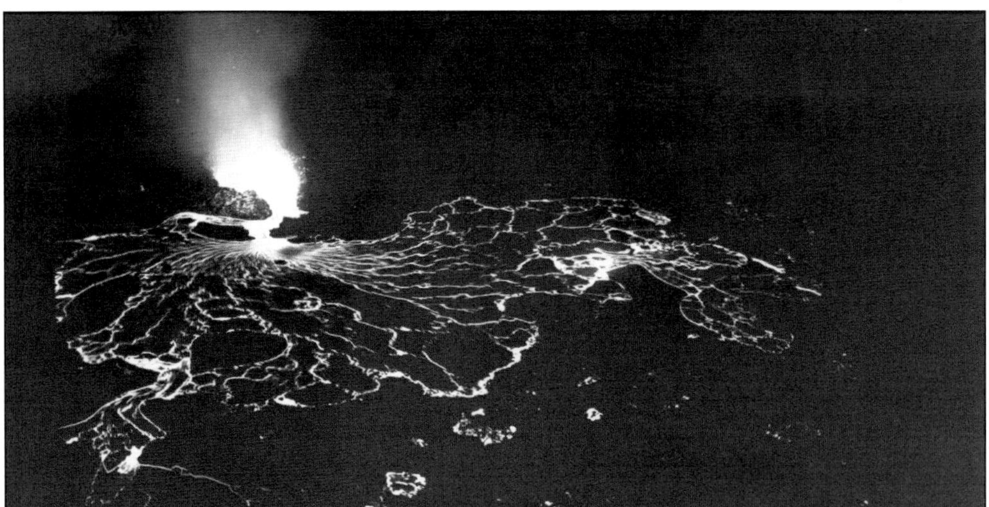

On September 11, 1934, during a national radio broadcast from the rim of Halemaumau, Thomas Jaggar—then director of the Hawaiian Volcano Observatory—described an eruption's fountains and lava flow as "indescribably beautiful, a vast labyrinth of glowing cobweb pattern ever changing radial and concentric to the central fountain group."

When Halemaumau erupted in September 1934, it ended a period of inactivity that had lasted for almost three years. This quiet period had been very bad for "Uncle" George Lycurgus, who bought Volcano House in 1932. When the volcano stopped erupting, the visitors stopped coming. In 1934, Lycurgus claimed that he was nearly bankrupt. With the help of Alec Lancaster, a local guide, Lycurgus hiked out to Halemaumau—the legendary home of Pele, the volcano goddess. There, the men prayed and left an offering of an ohelo berry lei (plus a partially empty bottle of gin that Lycurgus thought Pele would like), beseeching the goddess to please erupt.

"Uncle George" Lycurgus happily went to bed after his little talk with Pele. A few hours later, he—and the rest of the world—awoke to lava erupting from the floor of Halemaumau. Thousands of visitors came to view the 1934 eruption, and they filled Volcano House. Lycurgus told that story to many visitors over the years and professed his belief in Pele for the rest of his life.

During the 1934 eruption, lava fountains initially erupted from three points within Halemaumau Crater. Lava flows spread across the floor of Halemaumau and formed a glowing lake that quickly submerged the third, and most northern, line of fountains. Within hours, the entire crater floor was covered in 60 feet of lava.

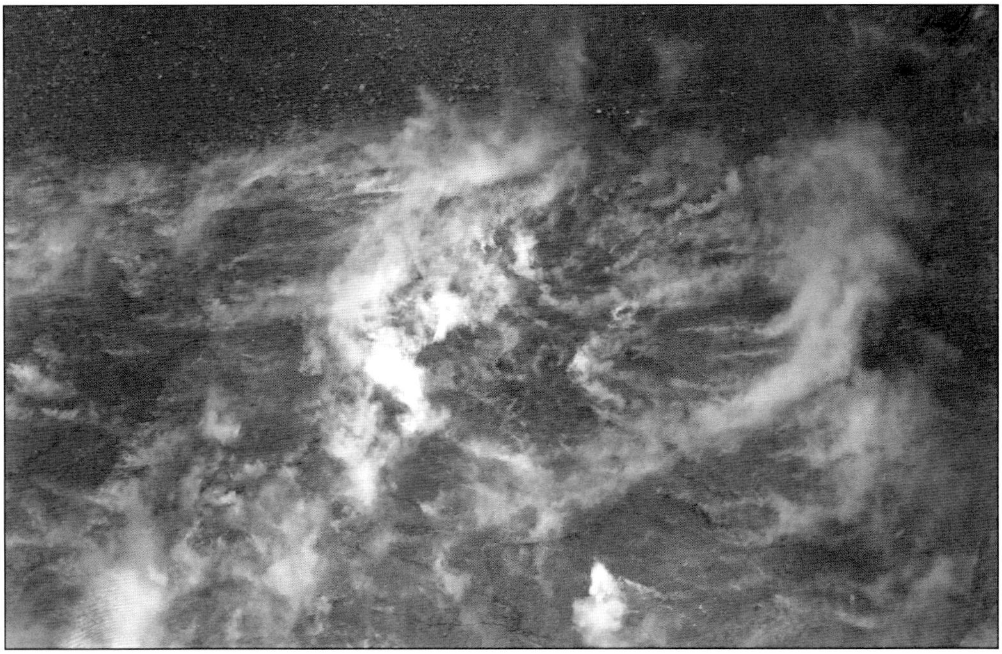

During the 1934 eruption, the vigorous lava fountains generated rumbling sounds that seemed to shake the whole volcano. At the same time, hot gases stirred up hundreds of whirlwinds and swept clouds of pumice and dust up to the western rim of Halemaumau. In the first 12 hours of the eruption, gas fumes rose several thousand feet into the air, filling the park with the odor of sulfur dioxide.

During the 1934 eruption, lava surged from a 900-foot horizontal crack that was located about halfway up the west wall of Halemaumau. Thirty jets of brilliant red lava shot up from the northwest crater floor, blowing fragments of pumice several hundred feet over the crater rim.

The west and northwest fountains of the 1934 eruption ceased to blow after about 12 hours, but the north fountains, located at the lava lake's center, persisted. The north fountains gradually dwindled, but lava continued to erupt from beneath the cooling surface of Halemaumau, oozing up through the cracks between the crater walls and the crust that covered the crater floor.

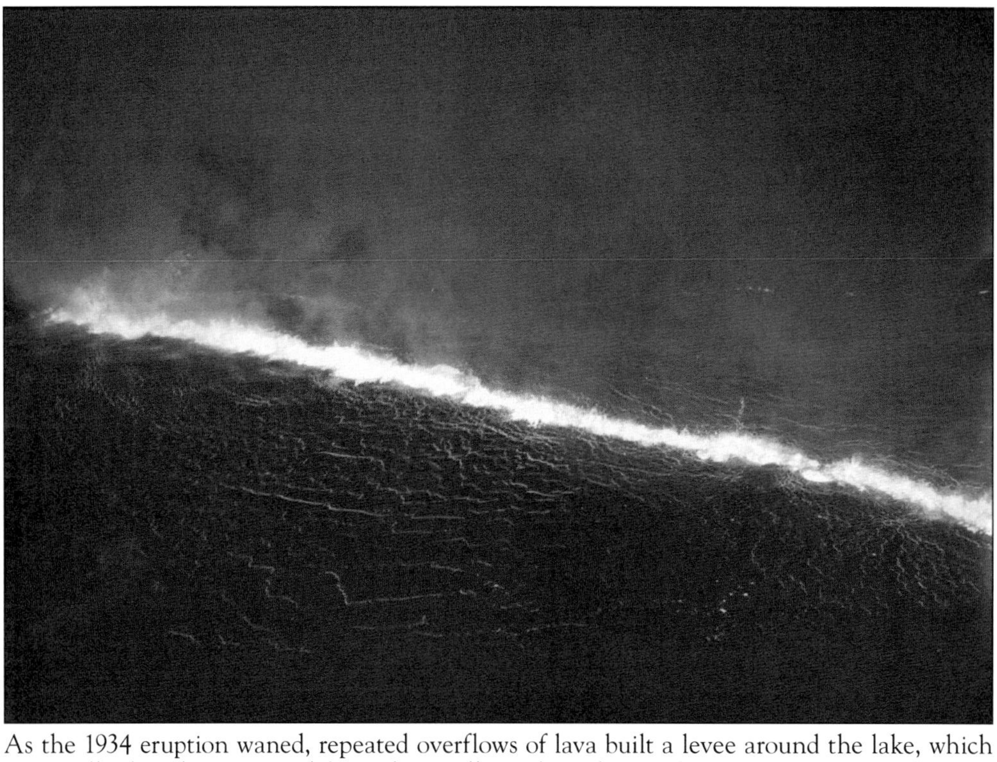

As the 1934 eruption waned, repeated overflows of lava built a levee around the lake, which eventually shrank in size and formed a small pond on the northeast side of the crater flood. Within the lake, lava welled up on the west side and drained on the east. Drainage episodes were accompanied by violent bursts of gas, producing loud noises that could be heard up to three miles away. After 30 minutes of complete silence, lava would stream back in and restore the lake.

When 1934's 33-day eruption finally ended, Pele began the longest period of inactivity in modern recorded history—18 years. On June 27, 1952, Pele again erupted in Halemaumau, and 93-year-old "Uncle George" Lycurgus was on the rim to watch it. Lycurgus still managed the Volcano House, and he was still a staunch believer in the volcano goddess.

On June 27, 1952, just a few minutes before midnight, a loud whistling noise pierced the air, and the night sky lit up with a bright orange glow. Kilauea had erupted again. Halemaumau Crater was nearly 800 feet deep at the time, but the fountain spewed so high that observers reported seeing the top of its plume above the crater rim.

During the 1952 eruption, most of the fountains reached heights of up to 100 feet. However, one fountain located near the bottom of the southwestern wall of the crater reached heights of up to 800 feet. This eruption certainly lived up to its name, as *kilauea* translates from the Hawaiian to "spewing" or "much spreading."

The 1952 eruption's lava fountains were accompanied by thick sulfurous fumes and rains of tephra (expelled materials that include ash, volcanic cinders, and rocks).

Before the 1952 eruption, geologists noticed cracks around the rim of Halemaumau Crater. Prior to this eruption, some people had taken the mountain's long silence as proof that Kilauea was dead. However, scientists took notice of frequent earthquakes, the occasional swelling and shrinking of the volcano, and the appearance of cracks and faults in the crater and along the rim. They knew that it was just a matter of time before Pele erupted again.

The 1952 eruption produced a continuous line—about 2,600 feet long—of lava fountains. They spread nearly the entire length of the crater floor, extended along the southwest and northeast walls, and reached partway up the northeastern crater wall.

During the 1952 eruption, visibility was poor inside of the crater due to a heavy fume, but small glimpses revealed that the older spatter cones on the crater floor had been buried under a rising lava lake. Scientists estimate that more than 3 million cubic meters of lava emerged during the first half hour of the eruption. Under Kilauea's current eruption conditions, it would take about six days for the east rift zone to produce that much lava.

Visibility was a problem for scientists during the 1952 eruption due to the heavy, sulfurous fume cloud and the rain of volcanic particles. One scientist had to have his car repainted—the falling pumice had sandblasted his vehicle. He also had to replace his windshield due to the hail of small rocks. The rate of eruption quickly declined after the initial outbreak, but lava fountains continued to spray across the surface of the lava lake for weeks. By the late summer of 1952, activity had begun to decline, but the eruption persisted until November 10, when, after 136 days, scientists observed the last fountain activity.

The seismograph in this picture shows the harmonic tremor that took place on November 5, 1967, signaling the start of a 251-day eruption. Kilauea's behavior during and between eruptions is remarkably regular. Monitoring instruments placed at the volcano's summit trace its cycles of gradual inflation, during which the reservoir fills with magma, and abrupt deflation, when the reservoir partially empties to deliver magma to an eruption. During inflation, the rocks surrounding the reservoir become stressed, and this stress is partly relieved by increasing numbers of earthquakes, which are too small to be felt but are easily recorded by seismographs at the Kilauea summit.

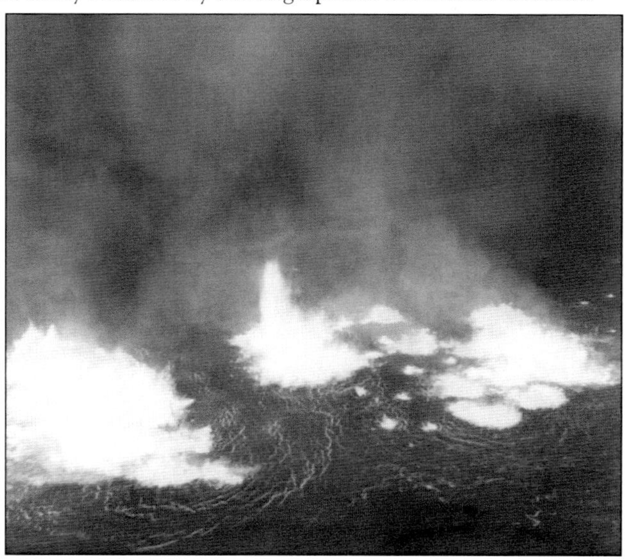

Just one hour after the seismographs lit up with earthquake activity, the November 5, 1967, eruption began. Although scientists are not yet able to predict eruptions, they have learned that when the volcano begins to inflate, followed by numerous earthquakes, an eruption is imminent. However, the question of "when" remains—will the volcano explode in an hour, a day, a week, or several weeks?

This photograph shows the eruption on November 5, 1967, when the Kilauea volcano began sending lava from vents on the floor of its 558-foot-deep summit pit crater, Halemaumau. The eruption ceased on July 13, 1968, after 31 separate phases of fountaining that were separated by short periods of quiescence. The eruptive phases pumped 110 million cubic yards of lava into Halemaumau Crater. Phases varied in duration and intensity, ranging from a low-key phase that lasted only eight hours to one that continued for 68 days. By phase 16, lava fountains were characterized by a massive bubbling rather than the tall bursts observed in earlier phases. The periods of quiet between eruptive phases varied in length from 12 hours to six days.

Seven

Changing Scenery

On January 3, 1983, Pele, the Hawaiian volcano goddess, sent incredibly hot gas and liquid lava up from the depths of the Kilauea volcano, ripping open a four-mile-long fissure in the east rift zone.

From Pu'u O'o, the fiery cone created by the eruption, roaring fountains of lava shot 1,500 feet into the air. These fountains could be heard for miles and signaled the start of an eruption that has lasted for decades and remains the longest eruption on record—perhaps the longest since the 15th century.

More than 30 years after Kilauea began its record-breaking eruption, some 500 acres of new land have been added to the island. However, two villages were destroyed, 215 homes were obliterated, eight miles of roads were buried under 82 feet of lava, a visitors' center at the Hawai'i Volcanoes National Park was covered by the eruption, and a 700-year-old Hawaiian temple (Waha'ulu Heiau) was destroyed.

Eruptions like this were once watched by ancient Hawaiian priests looking to appease the volcano goddess. Today, they are monitored by dozens of scientists, and all volcanic activity is tracked online, where it can be followed by millions of people around the world.

In the early days of the eruption, from 1983 to 1986, the Pu'u O'o vent exploded with lava every three to four weeks, but usually for less than 24 hours each time. The volcanic cone in Pu'u O'o had grown to 835 feet in height by mid-1986, as lava fountains erupted with aa lava—thick, blocky flows of rock-like magma.

In July 1986, the eruption moved two miles away to a new vent, Kupaianaha, and began producing smooth, flowing pahoehoe lava.

In March 1990, Pele's eruption turned destructive when lava flowed down toward the southeastern coast. There, it covered the rural subdivision of Kalapana Gardens, burying 100 homes under 80 feet of lava.

In 1991, lava flow from Kupaianaha was in decline. On February 7, 1992, it stopped completely. Ten days later, the eruption returned to Pu'u O'o, which erupted nearly continuously until 2003. Lava poured downslope, into the ocean, and continued to bury Kalapana Gardens. In January 1997, the crater floor of the volcano collapsed. On March 5, 2011, the nearby Kamoamoa fissure cracked open and released a curtain of lava that was 80 feet tall.

As this book goes to press in 2014, the eruption at Pu'u O'o continues with no end in sight.

After more than three decades of continuous eruptions at Kilauea, scientists have been able to gather copious amounts of data and now know quite a bit about the tectonic mechanics of how the volcano works. They know what types of earthquakes occur and have identified where the earthquakes occur and why, as well as the various types of gas emissions and what they indicate. Scientists estimate that Kilauea has been in a period of sporadic explosive eruptions for about 60 percent of that time, with the remaining 40 percent representing periods of quiet eruptions.

One reason that scientists have been able to study Kilauea is the number of instruments monitoring the volcano, including these seismometer lines set up in the Kau desert. These lines lead to the Hawaiian Volcano Observatory and help track earth movements, tilt, and other changes inside and outside the volcano. A thermal camera keeps watch on the lava lake and can "see" through the thick volcanic fume. Periodic laser scans of the crater and lava lake help track the evolving crater geometry. These tools—which include seismometers, tilt meters, GPS sensors, gas monitoring sensors, and webcams—are part of a robust monitoring network maintained by the observatory.

These hikers are walking the Kipuka Puaulu. This lush area is known as a *kipuka*, which is an area of land surrounded by lava flows. Occasionally, a lava flow splits and moves around an area of land, leaving it untouched. The Hawaiians called these areas *kipuka*, and they often resemble islands of diverse, flourishing vegetation amidst a sea of lava flows. The Kipuka Puaulu is a popular, easy hiking loop in Hawai'i Volcanoes National Park. It features a dirt trail with a gentle incline and enables visitors to see the dramatic contrast of lava flows and lush vegetation.

Most people think of destructive lava flows when they picture volcanic eruptions, but this photograph illustrates damage caused by the increased sulfur content of the air. Although the trees and grasses in this photograph were more than a half-mile from the eruption in Halemaumau Crater, the damage is severe. Long before the 1960 eruption buried the town of Kapoho, the sulfur fumes destroyed the papaya, coconut, orchid, and coffee farms surrounding the village.

Slow-moving lava crosses Chain of Craters Road in this 1986 photograph taken at Hawai'i Volcanoes National Park. Built in 1928, Chain of Craters Road was once a 23-mile paved road that wound through the east rift and coastal area of the park. In 1959, the road was lengthened to reach the tiny town of Kalapana. The road has been partially covered by lava several times due to eruptions of the Kilauea volcano. Lava flow closed the road in 1969, but it was reopened 10 years later. The flow pictured here caused another closure.

Before the 1983 eruption of Kilauea, people from across Hawaii, and scientists from around the world, raced to the Big Island to catch a glimpse of the eruption. This photograph, taken around the time of the 1967 Halemaumau eruption, shows how thousands of people flocked to the summit at Hawai'i Volcanoes National Park—braving howling winds, chilly weather, sulfur fumes, and the sting of wind-blown pumice and ash—for a front-row seat at Pele's creation of new earth.

In this image, fast-moving surface lava sparks fires in the grass and trees along a hillside trail. Between 1983 and 1990, the lava from the Kilauea eruption moved down the southern coast and destroyed everything in its path: homes, parks, roads, highways, and historical sites. The entire community of Kalapana was buried.

Here, park employee R.L. Barrel squats next to a "lava bomb"—a mass of molten rock larger than two and a half feet in diameter. Lava bombs are formed when they are ejected during an eruption, but they cool into solid rocks before they reach the ground. They can be quite dangerous, since they can be launched several feet at high velocity during an eruption. Also, due to internal gas pressure, they occasionally explode as they cool.

Some areas are severely damaged by heavy sulfur fumes even before surface lava arrives. Lava traveling in underground tubes, plus fast-moving fires in the grasses and trees, can also cause damage. This area of Puna, located far from the summit, was devastated well before the lava actually reached the area.

After a swarm of earthquakes, three sets of fissures opened in the Pauahi vent on November 16, 1979. The 22-hour eruption resulted in pahoehoe lava tumbling down the slope and crossing Chain of Craters Road, which was moved as a result of this eruption.

On November 15, 1979, numerous small earthquakes abruptly struck the upper east rift zone. At the peak of the event, the ground beneath Pauahi Crater (pictured) was shaken by as many as 20 earthquakes per hour. The earthquake swarm occurred along a 3.7-mile-long segment of the east rift zone. After the earthquakes began, the summit started to deflate, and at 8:18 a.m. on November 16, three sets of fissures shot lava fountains into the air. The eruption lasted for less than a day.

After allowing the pahoehoe lava to cool, a road crew inspects the damage to the lava-covered Chain of Craters Road. The road was covered by lava from flows from the Pu'u O'o eruption during a period from 1986 to 1991. Eight miles of the road had been covered with lava—much of it from the Kupaianaha vent. A nature trail was also covered, and in 1989, the Waha`ula Visitor Center, located on the south coast, was closed.

Here, lava cascades into Halemaumau from an outbreak halfway up the pit wall. This caused the lava lake to rise and eventually spill over the side before running down the slope.

During the 1979 eruption, a swarm of earthquakes at the summit may have caused this large crack in the road. All of the roads in the Hawai'i Volcanoes National Park are engaged in an open battle with Pele, and several have been covered with lava or cracked by earthquakes.

On rare occasions, the National Park Service has been able to remove cooled lava from roadways—if additional damage has not been done to the roads.

Eight

Volcano House

Volcano House, the oldest hotel in the Hawaiian Islands, is not located on a white sand beach. The gentle whisper of rolling surf is miles away. No palms trees sway outside the hotel's front doors.

The oldest hotel in Hawaii can trace its roots back to a grass shack believed to have been built on the orders of High Chiefess Kapiolani in 1844. Constructed in 1846, Volcano House sits at an elevation of 4,000 feet on the very rim of Kilauea—the most active volcano in the world.

Interestingly, one of the hotel's first reviews came from Mark Twain; after his 1866 trip to Volcano House, he reportedly quipped: "The surprise of finding a good hotel at such an outlandish spot startled me, considerably more than the volcano did."

Today, after numerous incarnations, the two-story, 33-room Volcano House—which is owned by the National Park Service and located in Hawai'i Volcanoes National Park—has allowed visitors to witness hundreds of eruptions through its floor-to-ceiling windows. Today, it continues to welcome adventuresome travelers and provide them with a comfortable place to bear witness to the work of Pele, the Hawaiian volcano goddess.

The location of Volcano House was first recorded in the journal of the missionary William Ellis, who described a trip he took in 1823 along with another missionary, Asa Thurston. Ellis told the Hawaiian guide that he did not like the location of the hut the guide had set up for them, as it was too close to the rim of the crater. The guide refused to move the hut, telling the missionaries that this was the only area where Pele allowed people to rest in safety.

The guide was right. The location, on the northeast side of the rim, is very safe. The prevailing northeastern trade winds keep gases away from this side of the crater, and the lava tends to flow away from the northeast side.

In 2010, the hotel closed for renovations and repairs. It reopened in 2013 after undergoing $4 million in upgrades, including seismic safety improvements.

This photograph shows the 1934 eruption drawing visitors to watch the fireworks from the rim in front of Volcano House. This is the same spot where Hawaiian Chiefess Kapiolani supposedly ordered the construction the first recorded temporary shelter on the mountain in 1844.

The chance for a bird's-eye view like this, from the beginning of the 1950 eruption, has continually drawn visitors to Volcano House. In 1846, Benjamin Pitman—a Hilo resident, sugarcane planter, and the husband of Hawaiian Chiefess Kino'ole—built the first permanent structure on the site where Volcano House now stands. Pitman's 1846 structure was a one-room thatched house with a fireplace. He named it Volcano House, and the name stuck. Pitman charged lodgers a nightly rate of $1 per person plus extra for meals.

A story in the August 16, 1860, *Pacific Commercial Advertiser* described Volcano House as measuring 12 feet by 18 feet, with no furniture inside and mats on the floor serving as beds for guests. This is a far cry from today's Volcano House, which features cabins, 33 guest rooms, and modern conveniences. This image is estimated to show Volcano House sometime around the 1950s.

Volcano House has gone through many incarnations over the years. In this photograph, ditches are being dug to install a new water line. A prominent incarnation of Volcano House was built in 1866, when Benjamin Pitman erected a wood-frame hotel to replace the original one-room structure. The new Volcano House had four guest rooms, a parlor, and a dining room. The writer Mark Twain stayed there and raved about the food he was served—a strawberry-fed goose (possibly a Hawaiian *nene*) that had been wrapped in leaves and baked in an *imu* pit.

For decades, Volcano House was the site of continuous construction, including the building of this protective wall facing the crater. In the late 19th century, the owners built one structure after another, and in 1877, a bigger, more modern hotel was built. The 1877 Volcano House was 101 by 36 feet, had six guest rooms, and can still be visited today, since this version of the hotel was declared a historic building before being relocated; it now serves as the Volcano Art Center. Numerous famous guests stayed at the 1877 Volcano House, including the writers Isabella Bird and Robert Louis Stevenson, King David Kalakaua, and French scientist Louis Pasteur.

Construction and landscaping seem to be constant at Volcano House. The hotel was rebuilt again in 1891, when a two-story Victorian-style building with 10 to 12 rooms was added to the 1877 structure. An observation tower was also added. During this period, Volcano House got a new manager: Peter Lee, a retired Norwegian sea captain. Lee had owned and managed another hotel in Hawaii and had also built a carriage road from Punaluu to Volcano Village. Lee was a well-loved manager who served from 1891 to 1898 and gained a reputation for never turning a guest away—even if it meant the guest had to sleep on the billiards table. Well-versed in the lore of the volcano, Lee gave nightly talks by the fireplace, which guests flocked to and loved.

Additional rooms were added to Volcano House in 1953. "Uncle" George Lycurgus is probably the best known of Volcano House's proprietors. Born in Sparta, Greece, in 1859, Lycurgus arrived in Hawaii in 1889 and became the manager of the San Souci Hotel in Waikiki. That hotel was sold in 1895 after Lycurgus was arrested for treason. He had hosted members of the failed 1895 counter-revolution, which supported the return of the deposed queen, Liliuokalani, to the throne. In 1904, Lycurgus acquired a controlling interest in Volcano House and became the manager of the property. He had a partial interest in the Volcano House Company from 1904 to 1921. In 1932, Lycurgus acquired sole ownership of the hotel for $300 at an auction in Hilo; he held the ownership until around 1941, when the National Park Service purchased the hotel. He managed the hotel until his death in 1960 at age 101.

As visitors gather on the rim of the crater in front of Volcano House, few may realize that in 1912, Massachusetts Institute of Technology professor Dr. Thomas Jaggar had realized the advantages of studying a volcano on-site—as it was erupting—and built his science observatory adjacent to the hotel. Uncle George Lycurgus's family raised the money to build a small structure next to the hotel to house Jaggar's scientific instruments, and by February 1912, workers had begun construction on Jaggar's Hawaiian Volcano Observatory. Jaggar resided there for the next 28 years, often giving scientific talks to hotel guests. In the early 1940s, the observatory was moved to a new building 200 yards away from the caldera rim. In 1948, the observatory moved again, this time to a building at the top of Uwekahuna Bluff (located on the northwest rim of Kilauea caldera). Finally, it occupied a new, larger building on the same site in 1986. As director of the Hawaiian Volcano Observatory, Jaggar became a pioneer in the relatively new science of volcanology.

After a decade of lobbying by Lorrin A. Thurston, Dr. Thomas A. Jaggar, and numerous others in Hawaii, the area surrounding Kilauea finally became a national park when Pres. Woodrow Wilson signed the country's 13th national park into existence on August 1, 1916. When the document was signed, the new park, then called Hawaii National Park, consisted of the summits of Kilauea and Mauna Loa on Hawaii island and the summit of Haleakala on Maui. Eventually, Kilauea caldera was added to the park, followed by the forests of Mauna Loa, the Kau Desert (the site of the ancient warrior footprints), the Ola'a Rainforest, and the Kalapana archaeological area in the Puna/Kau Historic District. In 1961, Haleakala became a separate national park (Haleakala National Park). Over the years, various areas have been added to Hawai'i Volcanoes National Park, which now encompasses 333,086 square miles on the island of Hawaii.

In 1921, the Inter-Island Steam Navigation Company brought the Volcano House property, providing transportation to the island, transportation to the hotel, and a stay at the hotel in one package deal. That same year, the company built a new, modernized, two-story wing to replace the 1877 structure, which was then relocated to its current location. In this period, visitors to Volcano House included Jack London, Pres. Franklin D. Roosevelt (who visited in 1934, making him the first US president to visit Hawaii), Amelia Earhart, and Princess Victoria Kaiulani.

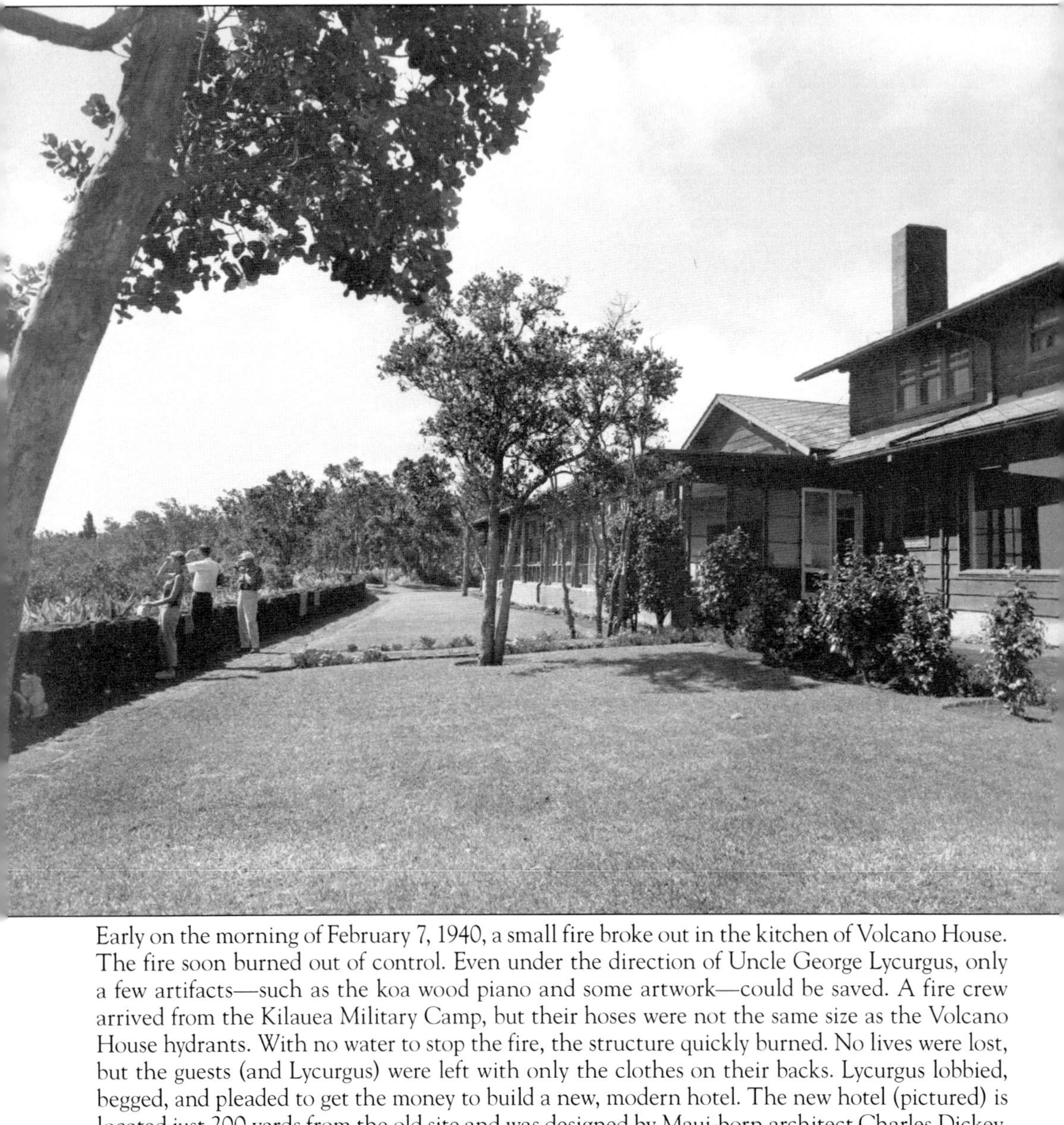

Early on the morning of February 7, 1940, a small fire broke out in the kitchen of Volcano House. The fire soon burned out of control. Even under the direction of Uncle George Lycurgus, only a few artifacts—such as the koa wood piano and some artwork—could be saved. A fire crew arrived from the Kilauea Military Camp, but their hoses were not the same size as the Volcano House hydrants. With no water to stop the fire, the structure quickly burned. No lives were lost, but the guests (and Lycurgus) were left with only the clothes on their backs. Lycurgus lobbied, begged, and pleaded to get the money to build a new, modern hotel. The new hotel (pictured) is located just 200 yards from the old site and was designed by Maui-born architect Charles Dickey. It originally had 24 rooms, but more were added between 1958 and 1961.

The floor-to-ceiling windows in the dining room and lounge of Volcano House provide visitors with a close view of any eruptions.

On February 8, 1940, the day after a fire destroyed Volcano House, the *Hawaii Tribune-Herald* ran the headline: "Volcano House Reopened Today." It was an optimistic statement, but it fit with "Uncle" George Lycurgus's determination to keep the hotel going. He moved guests into the old 1877 Volcano House, returning it to service as a hotel. Several freestanding cottages were unharmed by the fire, and they also served as housing for the displaced guests.

The new Volcano House—paid for by the National Park Service—opened on November 8, 1941, and was designed by well-known Hawaii architect Charles William Dickey. Dickey's work is very distinctive, and the shape of the roof and projecting eaves became such a trademark that the style became locally known as the "Dickey roof." Many other architects have adopted this style over the years, and it has now become a stereotypical feature of contemporary Hawaiian architecture.

After the new Volcano House (pictured) opened in 1941, the 1877 structure was converted into staff housing. For a brief period during World War II, the building was used as a bar and casino for servicemen from the Kilauea Military Camp. When the war was over, the building returned to use as a staff dormitory until 1972, when it was abandoned. In 1974, it reopened as the Volcano Art Center.

Today, the 33-room Volcano House hotel is owned by the National Park Service and managed by the Hawaii Volcanoes Lodge Company. The NPS purchased the hotel around 1941, after a 1940 fire destroyed most of the original structure. The NPS closed it in 2010 for complete renovation, including two new decks overlooking Kilauea crater. The hotel reopened in 2013.

The park also offers cabins and camping at the Namakani Paio campgrounds. Managed by the Hawaii Volcano Lodge Company, these 10 A-frame cabins and 16 campsites are available for rent. Nestled in a eucalyptus grove just three miles from Volcano House and located at an elevation of 4,000 feet, the campground provides a unique experience. The cabins, which were recently refurbished with new flooring and beds, sleep four and come equipped with two bunk beds and a twin bed.

When word gets out about a new eruption, like this 1952 curtain of fire, the phones explode at Volcano House as people across the state make plans to see the volcano.

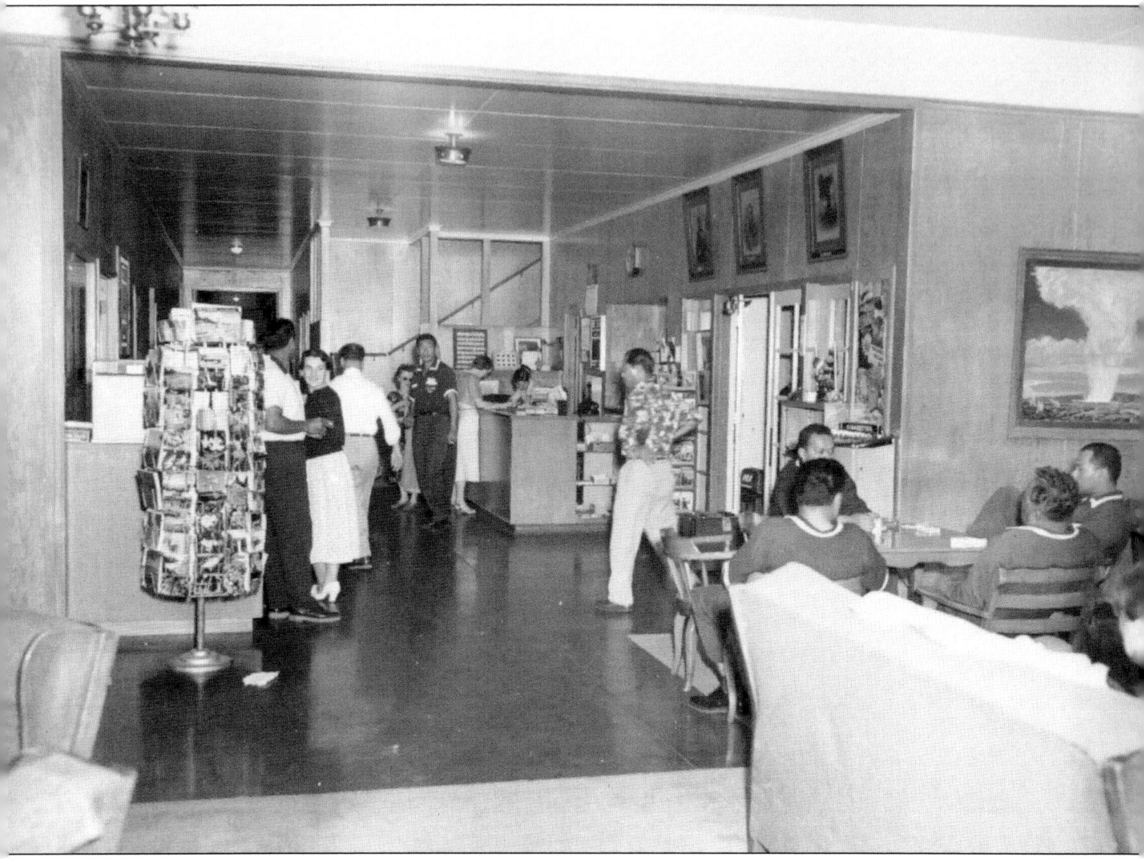

This is the lobby at Volcano House as it appeared before the 2010 renovations. Because of the building's historic designation, all renovations must first be approved by Hawaii's Historical Preservation Division. For example, the hotel's floors remained polished concrete in keeping with the original design of the 1941 building.

The entrance to Volcano House may have changed over the years, but the original lava rock fireplace still warms the lobby in the chilly, high-elevation evenings. Inside, a polished concrete floor the color of deep jade still carries its 1940s luster, and visitors are still greeted by an imposing bronze sculpture—created by Honolulu artist Marguerite Blassingame—of the volcano goddess Pele.

On the side of the hotel that faces the rim of the crater, floor-to-ceiling windows look out over the caldera, providing a spectacular view of eruptions.

Throughout its journey from a grass shack to a one-room wood structure to an energy-efficient hotel designed by a noted architect, Volcano House has provided visitors with a place to rest since 1846. Visitors have included royalty, presidents, and celebrities. The Hawaiian queen Liliuokalani even visited the hotel on December 9, 1874.

So many people flock to see the Halemaumau eruptions that the park was forced to build a viewing stand. The volcano erupted three times in 1961—on February 24, March 3, and July 10. It then erupted again for almost all of 1967.

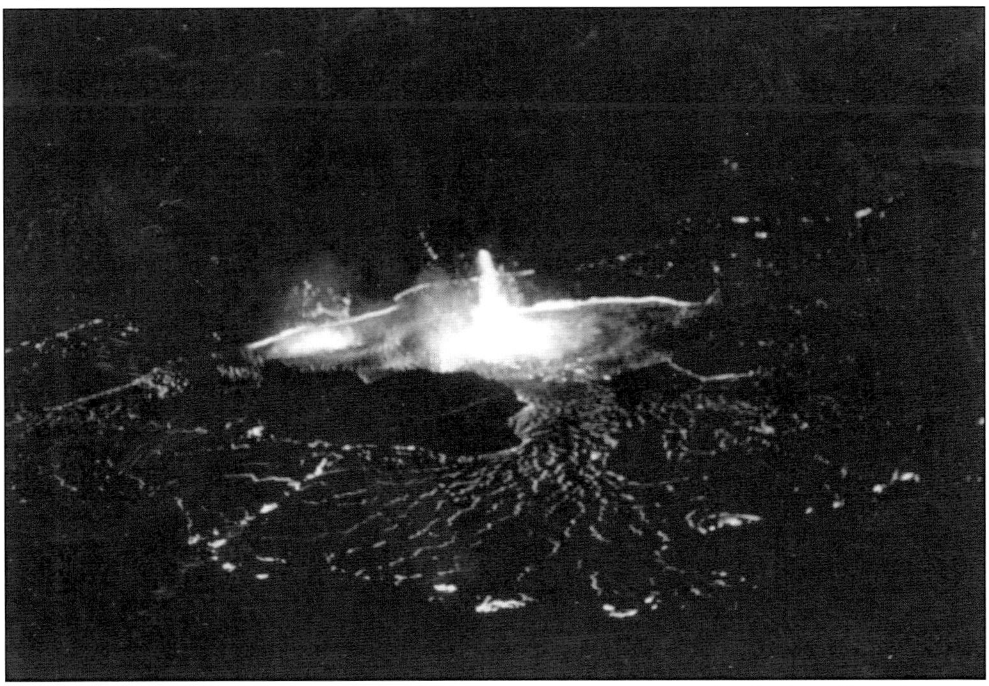

On June 27, 1952, just before midnight, Kilauea erupted in a spectacular display of lava shooting over the rim of the crater. This magnificent show drew people from all over the state to watch the display, which ended after 136 days.

On August 22, 1968, an eruption from the east rift zone made a big blast but only lasted for five days. On October 7 that same year, it erupted again.

The November 14, 1959, eruption on the floor of the Kilauea Iki crater produced a large volume of lava during its short, 36-day eruption.

The view from Volcano House's floor-to-ceiling windows is as memorable as the food in the dining room. The hotel restaurant serves locally sourced meals like Big Island lamb rubbed with Hilo coffee, *opakapaka* wrapped in white pineapple slices, and an avocado and mango dip served with homemade root-vegetable chips.

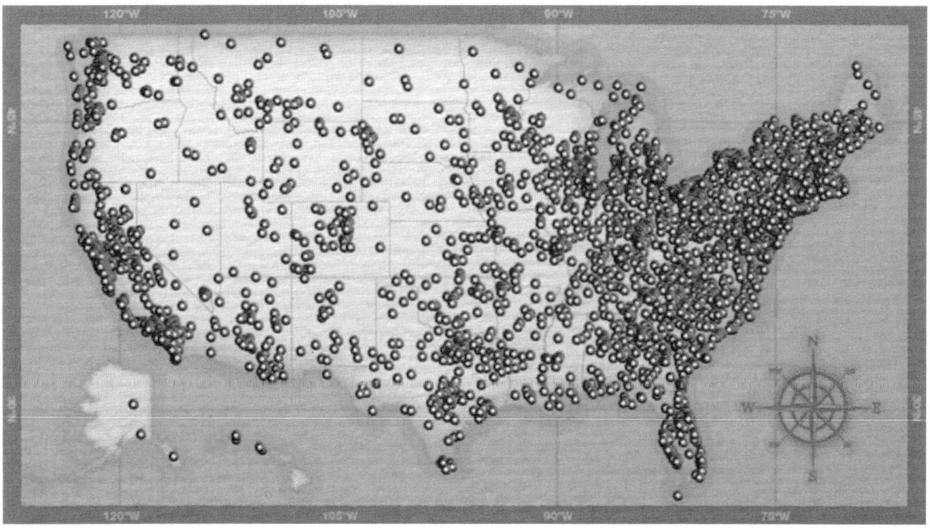